THE PERFECTION LEARNING
PARALLEL TEXT SERIES

Early American Literature

Perfection Learning® Corporation
Logan, Iowa 51546-0500

Editorial Director: Julie A. Schumacher
Writer: Diane Faith Eickhoff
Design: Kay Ewald

Cover Art:
The Nation Makers by Howard Pyle, Collection of the
Brandywine River Museum, Purchased through a
grant from the Mabel Pew Myrin Trust

Images used in this book are copyright www.
arttoday.com, Corel, and the Library of Congress.

Paperback ISBN 0-7891-5325-4
Cover Craft® ISBN 0-7807-9712-4

5 6 PP 06 05

Using This Parallel Text

This collection of American literature classics is especially designed for readers who may not be accustomed to the formal English of America's early writers. The original text for each selection is found on the left-hand page while a modern English version is located on the right. Matching numbers help you keep track as you move back and forth between the two versions.

If you are having difficulty with the original text, try reading a passage of the modern version first. Then read the same passage in its original form. After a while, you may find that the original text becomes easier to understand, and that you rely on the modern text less and less.

In any case, remember that the modern paraphrase should never be used as a substitute for the original. While you may not plan on becoming a literary scholar, as an educated person, it is important to have some familiarity with early American writers and their ideas. Keep in mind that these authors were not stuffy, dried-up old men and women, they were passionate, powerful users of language who cared deeply about the issues of their day. The fact that you now sit in a classroom in a united, democratic country with liberty and justice for all is largely due to the stirring voices of the writers represented in this book.

Table of Contents

Unit Three **A Growing Nation** (1800–1870)

Unit One
Beginnings
(to 1750)

Before Europeans discovered America for themselves, American Indians lived and flourished throughout both North and South America for more than 20,000 years. American Indians were in Hispaniola (now the Dominican Republic) when Christopher Columbus landed there in 1492.

The Spaniards

Stories of Columbus's voyages encouraged other Spanish explorers. Over the next century, many expeditions crossed the Atlantic, led by men like Cortés, De Soto, and Coronado. American Indians played a role in most of these explorations. They guided expeditions, aided communications, and taught the newcomers survival skills. Nevertheless, the Indians were often treated badly, and whole civilizations were wiped out by war and diseases.

Some of the Spanish explorers kept written accounts of their adventures and exploits. From these early narratives we have the first impressions of Europeans on the continent. One of the most interesting of these is a report by Álvar Núñez Cabeza de Vaca, the leader of a small band of Spaniards who survived shipwreck and other trials. The excerpt from *La Relación*

(*The Report*) that is included in this unit shows how Cabeza de Vaca interacted with some of the Indians he met on his amazing trek across the Americas.

The Puritans

Unlike the Spanish who brought primarily soldiers and missionaries, the English came in shiploads of men, women, and children. They wanted a new life in a new land far away from their old homes. The first English settlement in Jamestown, Virginia, in 1607, was almost wiped out in its first winter. Had it not been for the assistance of helpful Indians, the settlement would have perished.

The same was true of another group of Puritans who attempted to land in Virginia but ended up at the tip of what is now Cape Cod, Massachusetts, in 1620. We know them as the Pilgrims who sailed on the *Mayflower*. They were also called Puritans because they had tried to "purify" the Church of England. Far from being thanked for their efforts, they were persecuted and driven from England to Holland. After a few years they decided to sail for the New World. Here they hoped they could worship God as they pleased.

The Puritans elected a serious young man, William Bradford, to be governor of their settlement. Bradford, whose wife had drowned tragically just as Bradford and some of the other men were going ashore, was an able and respected leader of the new colony. He was governor for the next 33 years. During that time he wrote a history of the new settlement called *Of Plymouth Plantation*, a portion of which is included in this unit. In his book Bradford described how Indians, and in particular one Indian named Squanto, helped the Puritans survive their first year. Bradford's history is a valuable firsthand account of the new colony.

The religious beliefs of the Pilgrims, or Puritans, were narrow and strict. They believed in a stern, just God who punished sinners and rewarded the chosen few with eternal life. Along with godliness, they believed in hard work, honesty, a clean and sober lifestyle, and thrift. These traits helped them survive in the wilderness of their adopted home.

Though the Puritans did not believe in worldly pursuits, they did believe in education. They were, in fact, well-educated for their time. How else would the faithful be able to read their Bibles? Harvard College was opened in 1636 to make sure that the ministers of the church received a solid education. A number of Puritans were gifted writers and poets. Anne Bradstreet and Edward Taylor, whose poems are part of this unit, would have been called fine poets anywhere. Bradstreet's poems are optimistic, elegant, and passionate. She is our first American poet. Edward Taylor's poems are considered the equal of poets in Europe at the time.

After other Protestant groups arrived in America, the Puritan religion began to lose its hold on many people. The Great Awakening (1735–1750) was a religious revival in the colonies that tried to bring people who were starting to stray back to the fold. Jonathan Edwards, a brilliant and well-educated minister with an ability to paint dramatic pictures of heaven and hell, became one of the best-known leaders of the revival. Edwards' fiery sermons were meant to put the fear of God into people, as you will see when you read "Sinners in the Hands of an Angry God" in this unit. Despite the efforts of Edwards and others, however, the number of Puritans in America got smaller and smaller.

Most of the writings from the Puritans in New England are religious writings or histories. Even the histories have religious overtones because everything in life was supposed to reflect the glory of God. If a piece of writing was just for fun, it was considered a waste of time—or a work of the devil. The Puritans had an enormous influence on America that is still felt today. When people talk about core values or the "faith of our fathers" or a return to morality, they are referring—often without knowing it—to the Puritans.

Unit One Author Biographies

Álvar Núñez Cabeza de Vaca 1490–1557

Álvar Núñez Cabeza de Vaca was one of the early Spanish explorers of the Americas. With a small band of men, Cabeza de Vaca crossed both Americas on foot looking for treasure. He wrote what might be considered the earliest tour guide of the Americas. *La Relación* (*The Report*), from which the excerpt in this unit is taken, is the record of his eight years of travel and exploration. It gives today's readers an amazing account of both his adventures and his thoughts about those adventures and the Native Americans he met along the way.

William Bradford 1590–1657

William Bradford was one of the original Pilgrims who came to America from England on the *Mayflower* in 1620. He was a deeply religious man whose beliefs led to persecution in England, exile in Holland, and a deep longing to live in a place where he and others like him could worship as they pleased. His leadership abilities were recognized early on, and he was elected governor of the Pilgrims' first settlement, Plymouth Colony. In that post, which he held for over 30 years, he was judge and jury, superintendent of agriculture and trade, and the person who allotted land to other Puritans. All of these roles gave him a unique perspective on the new colony. Ten years after landing on Plymouth Rock, Bradford began writing a history of the colony, *Of Plymouth Plantation*. Bradford's history has been read and re-read by every generation of students because it gives an accurate firsthand account of the Pilgrims' early years.

Anne Bradstreet 1612–1672

Anne Bradstreet is not only the best-known Puritan poet, she was also the first American poet to receive recognition in England. Bradstreet's poems are still admired today for their grace and beauty. Though she came from a noble family, she adapted well to life in a wilderness lacking the comforts of life she had experienced in England. Her elegant poems give us a glimpse into the private world of a deeply committed, loving, spiritual, and intelligent Puritan woman.

Edward Taylor   c. 1642–1729

Edward Taylor came to the colonies as a young man to avoid taking an oath of allegiance to the Church of England. He was educated for the ministry at Harvard University and spent his life serving a parish in Westfield, Massachusetts. At the time, Westfield was the western frontier of what would become the United States. Only two stanzas of one of Taylor's poems were published during his lifetime. Probably out of a sense of modesty or piety, Bradford told his heirs to not publish any of his poems after his death. Fortunately, the poems were filed away at Yale University and rediscovered in 1939.

Jonathan Edwards   1703–1758

Jonathan Edwards was a brilliant Puritan preacher. At 13 he was admitted to Yale University where he learned about the great philosophical ideas of the time. Many of them were opposed to his own religious beliefs as a strict Puritan. Edwards became famous as a preacher at revival meetings during a time in colonial history known as the Great Awakening (1733–1750). He put the fear of God into his listeners with sermons such as "Sinners in the Hands of an Angry God." Though he was later dismissed from his congregation for being too strict, he is remembered today as the best example of Puritan religious thought.

La Relación

Álvar Núñez Cabeza de Vaca

C La relacion que dio Aluar nu-
ñez cabeça de vaca de lo acaescido enlas Indias
enla armada donde yua por gouernador Pā
philo de narbaez desde el año de veynti
y siete hasta el año d treynta y seys
que boluio a Seuilla con tres
de su compañia.:.

1   And so we sailed on together for four days, eating a ration of a half-handful of raw maize daily. At the end of these four days we were overtaken by a storm that caused us to lose sight of the other boat, and through God's great mercy toward us we did not all founder, so bad was the weather, and with its being winter and very cold and the hunger we had suffered for so many days. As a result of the buffeting we received from the sea, next day the men began to fail very much, so that by sun-

2 set all those in my boat were lying heaped upon one another, so near to death that few of them were conscious, and by this time not five men among them were fit to stand. And when night fell only the mate and I were capable of sailing the boat, and two hours after nightfall the mate told me to take over, for he was in such a condition that he thought he would die

La Relación

Álvar Núñez Cabeza de Vaca

Álvar Núñez Cabeza de Vaca left Spain on June 17, 1527, as treasurer of an expedition that consisted of five ships and 600 men. Their goal was to "conquer and govern the provinces that lie between the River Las Palmas and the tip of Florida." For the next year and a half the expedition suffered through storms, shipwrecks, starvation, disease, and battles with American Indians. The following excerpt from Cabeza de Vaca's La Relación *(The Report) begins as he and about forty other men in a handmade boat sail in the Gulf of Mexico looking for land.*

1   *A*nd so we sailed on together for four days. Our food ration was a half-handful of raw corn daily. At the end of these four days we were overtaken by a storm that caused us to lose sight of the other boat. Through God's great mercy our boat did not fill with water and sink, though the weather was bad. It was winter and very cold, and we were hungry for many days. As a result of being beat upon by the sea, the men were totally exhausted.

2   By sunset of the next day all of the men in my boat were lying in a heap, so near to death that only a few of them were conscious. Less than five of the men were able to stand at this point. When night came, only the mate and I were capable of sailing the boat. Two hours after nightfall the mate told me to take over because he was in such bad shape that he

that night. And so I took the helm, and after midnight I went to see if the mate was dead, and he told me that he was in fact better and that he would steer until morning.

3   At that moment I would surely have much preferred to accept death than see so many people before my eyes in such a condition. And after the mate took charge of the boat I rested a little, but very restlessly, and nothing was further from my thoughts than sleep. Near dawn I thought I heard breakers, for as the coast was low the waves made a great deal of noise, and called to the mate in alarm; he answered that he thought we were near land, and we made soundings and found a depth of seven fathoms, and he thought we ought to stay at sea until daylight. And so I took an oar and rowed parallel to the land, for we were a league away from it, and then turned our stern to the sea. And when we were near land a

4   wave took us that tossed the boat out of the water a good horseshoe's cast; and with the great jolt it gave, almost all the men in the boat who were half dead came to themselves. And as they saw that land was near, they began to slip over the side and crawl on hands and feet, and as they came ashore where there were some gullies, we made a fire and cooked some maize that we had with us and found some rainwater; and with the heat of the fire the men revived and began to recover their spirits somewhat. The day we arrived there was the sixth of November.

5   After the men had eaten I sent Lope de Oviedo, who was stronger and hardier than anyone else, to go to some trees that were nearby and climb one of

thought he would die that night. And so I took the helm,[1] and after midnight I went to see if the mate was dead. He told me that he was, in fact, better and that he would steer until morning.

3   At that moment I would have rather died than seen so many people in such terrible shape. After the mate took charge of the boat I rested a little, but uneasily. Nothing was further from my thoughts than sleep. Near dawn I thought I heard breakers,[2] for the coast was low and the waves made a great deal of noise. I called to the mate in alarm, and he answered that he thought we were near land. We took measurements and found a depth of seven fathoms.[3] He thought we ought to stay at sea until daylight. I took an oar and rowed parallel to the land, for we were about a league[4] away from shore. I then turned our stern[5] to the sea.

4   When we were near land a wave tossed the boat out of the water a good horseshoe's toss. The great jolt woke up almost all of the half-dead men. When they saw that land was near, they began to slip over the side and crawl on their hands and feet. As we came ashore we found some gullies where we made a fire, cooked some corn that we had with us, and found rainwater. The heat of the fire began to revive the men, and they regained their spirits a bit. The day we arrived there was November 6th.

5   After the men had eaten I sent Lope de Oviedo, who was stronger and healthier than anyone else, to go climb some nearby trees in order to get an idea of

1 **helm:** the steering gear of a ship
2 **breaker:** wave, usually near the shore, that breaks into foam
3 **fathom:** about six feet
4 **league:** about three nautical miles
5 **stern:** the rear end of a ship

them, to find out what sort of country we were in and try to gain some idea of it. He did this and realized that we were on an island and saw that the earth on the mainland was trampled like the ground where livestock have often passed, and this made him think that it was Christian territory, and he told us so. I told him to go and look again more carefully, and to see if there were paths there that could be followed, but not to go too far away because of possible danger. He went and, finding a path, walked along it for about half a league and found some Indian huts that were empty because the Indians had gone out into the countryside; and he took one of their pots and a little dog and a few mullet and came back to us.

❊ ❊ ❊

6   And as we thought him long in returning, I sent two other Christians to look for him and find out what had happened to him, and they caught sight of him nearby and saw that three Indians with bows and arrows were following him and calling to him, and he was answering them by signs.

7   And so he reached the place where we were and the Indians stayed a short distance behind, seated right on the shore; and after half an hour a hundred other Indians armed with arrows came, who whether they were large or not seemed like giants owing to our fear, and they stopped near us, where the first three were. As for us, it was useless to think that anyone could defend himself, for there were scarcely half a dozen who could get up from the ground. The inspector and I went toward them and called to them and they came closer to us; and as best we could we tried to reassure them and ourselves and gave them beads and hawk's bells, and each of them gave me an

what sort of country we were in. He did this and
realized that we were on an island. He saw that the
earth on the mainland was flattened as if by livestock. This made him think that it was Christian
territory, and he told us so. I told him to go and look
again more carefully to see if there were paths that
could be followed, but not to go too far away because
of possible danger. He went, and finding a path,
walked along it for about half a league. He found
some Indian huts that were empty because the
Indians had gone out into the countryside. He took
one of their pots and a little dog and a few fish and
came back to us.

6   Because he had been gone a long time, I sent two
other Christians to look for him and find what had
happened to him. They caught sight of him nearby
and saw that three Indians with bows and arrows
were following him and calling to him, and he was
answering them in sign language.

7   And so he reached the place where we were while
the Indians stayed a short distance behind, seated on
the shore. After half an hour a hundred other Indians
came, armed with arrows. Because of our fear they
seemed like giants, whether they were large or not.
They stopped near us, where the first three Indians
were. It was useless to think that any man could
defend himself, for there were only half a dozen of us
who could get up from the ground. The inspector and
I went toward them and called to them. As they came
closer to us, we tried our best to reassure them and
ourselves and gave them beads and hawk's bells.
Each of them gave me an arrow, a sign of friendship.

arrow, which is a sign of friendship; and they told us by signs that they would return in the morning and bring us food, for at the moment they had none.

8   Next day as the sun was rising, which was the hour that the Indians had indicated to us, they came to us as they had promised and brought us a large quantity of fish and some roots that they eat and that resemble nuts, some larger and some smaller; most of them are gathered underwater, and with much effort. In the afternoon they returned and brought us more fish and the same roots and had their women and children come to see us, and so they returned rich with the bells and beads that we gave them, and on other days they visited us again with the same things as before. As we saw that we were
9   well supplied with fish and roots and water and the other things that we asked them for, we decided to launch the boats again and continue on our way; and we dug the boat out of the sand in which it was half buried, and we all had to strip and expend a great deal of effort to get it into the water, for we were in such a sorry plight that even much lighter tasks exhausted us. And so, having launched the boat, we were a distance of two crossbow shots into the sea when there came a wave so huge that it soaked us all, and as we were naked and the cold was so great, we let go of the oars, and another wave from the sea overturned the boat. The inspector and two others clung to it to escape death: but quite the opposite happened, for the boat carried them under and they were drowned.

10   As the coast there is very rugged, the sea in one lurch threw all the others, submerged in the waves and half drowned, onto the shore of the same island, and the only ones missing were the three whom the boat had carried under. The rest of us who escaped

They told us by sign language that they would return in the morning with food, but at the moment they didn't have any.

8   The next day as the sun was rising, the Indians came to us as promised and brought a large amount of fish and some large and small roots. These roots that they eat resemble nuts and are gathered underwater with much effort. In the afternoon they returned and brought us more fish and the same roots. This time they brought their women and children along to see us and returned rich with the bells and beads that we gave them. On other days they visited us again with the same things as before.

9   When we saw that we had a good supply of fish, roots, water, and the other things we asked them for, we decided to launch the boats again and continue on our way. We dug the boat out of the sand in which it was half buried. We all had to strip off our clothes and work hard to get the boat into the water. We were in such weak physical condition that even much easier tasks exhausted us. We launched the boat and were a distance of two crossbow shots into the sea when a huge wave came and soaked us all. Because we were naked and it was so cold, we let go of the oars. Then another wave came and overturned our boat. The inspector and two other men clung to the boat to escape death, but the opposite happened. The boat carried them under, and they drowned.

10   The coast at that point is very rugged, and in one lurch the sea threw all the rest of us half-drowned men onto the shore of the same island we had just left. The only ones missing were the three whom the boat had carried under. The rest of us who escaped

were naked as the day we were born and had lost all that we had with us, which though it was not worth much, was everything to us at that time. And since by then it was November and the cold was very great and we were in such a plight that one could have counted our bones without difficulty, we looked like the very image of death. Of myself I can say that I had eaten nothing but roasted maize since the month of May, and sometimes I had to eat it raw, for though the horses were slaughtered during the time the boats were being built, I was never able to eat them and did not eat fish as many as ten times.

11   I say this to avoid entering into further explanations, for anyone can imagine the sorry state we were in. And in addition to everything I have said, a north wind had started to blow, so that we were closer to death than to life. But it pleased Our Lord that, as we searched among the embers of the fire we had made there, we found fire, with which we made great bonfires, and thus we were imploring Our Lord for mercy and pardon for our sins, shedding many tears, each one bewailing not only his own plight but that of all the others whom he saw in

12   the same state. And at the hour of sunset the Indians, believing that we had not left, came looking for us again to bring us food; but when they saw us in such different circumstances as at first, and in such a strange condition, they were so frightened that they turned back. I went toward them and called them and they came, in great consternation; I gave them to understand by signs how a boat had sunk and three of our number had drowned, and there before them they saw two corpses and saw that those of us who were left were on the way to

13   becoming corpses too. When the Indians saw the disaster that had come upon us and the disaster we were in, with so much ill luck and misery, they sat

were naked as the day we were born and lost all that we had with us. Even though it was not worth much, it meant everything to us. It was November and very cold. We looked like the very picture of death; you could have counted our ribs without difficulty. I had eaten nothing but roasted corn since the month of May. Sometimes I had to eat it raw. Though the horses were slaughtered during the time the boats were being built, I was never able to eat them, nor did I eat fish even ten times.

11   I say this to avoid further explanations. Anyone can imagine the terrible state we were in. In addition to everything I have said, a north wind began to blow, and we were closer to death than to life. But by the grace of God, as we searched among the embers of the fire we had made there, we found fire. With it we made huge bonfires. We begged God for mercy and forgiveness for our sins and cried many tears. Each one of us was weeping not only for his own situation, but for the others as well.

12   At sunset the Indians, who thought we had not left, came looking for us again to bring us food. When they saw us in such a wretched state, they were so frightened that they turned back. I went toward them and called them. They came in great dismay. I helped them understand through sign language how our boat had sunk and three of our group had drowned. They saw two corpses and realized that those of us who were left were on the way to becoming corpses too.

13   When the Indians realized the disaster that had come upon us and all the bad luck and misery we had seen, they felt great grief and pity. They sat

down among us and, with the great grief and pity they felt on seeing us in such a desperate plight, all of them began to weep loudly, and so sincerely that they could be heard a long way off, and this lasted more than half an hour; and certainly, to see that those uncivilized and savage men, like brutes, were so sorry for us, caused me and others in our company to feel still more grief and the full realization of our misfortune.

✳ ✳ ✳

14   When this weeping had subsided I questioned the Christians and said that if they were in agreement I would ask those Indians to take us to their houses; and some of them, who had been in New Spain, answered that there could be no question of it, for if they took us to their houses they would sacrifice us to their idols. But in view of the fact that there was no other solution, and that if we took any other course death would be closer and more certain, I paid no heed to what they were saying; rather, I implored the Indians to take us to their houses, and they showed great pleasure at the prospect and told us to wait for a little while and they would do as we wished; and then thirty of them loaded themselves with firewood and went to their houses, which were a good distance away; and we stayed with the others

15   until near nightfall, when they seized us, and holding us closely and in great haste, went with us to their houses. And because it was very cold, and fearing that some of us might die or collapse on the way, they provided four or five very large bonfires placed at intervals and warmed us at each one; and as soon as they saw that we had acquired some strength and warmth they took us to the next fire, so quickly that they scarcely allowed our feet to touch the ground,

down among us and began to weep so loudly and so sincerely that they could be heard a long way off. This went on more than half an hour. Seeing those uncivilized savages feel such pity for us caused me and the others in our group to feel even more grief. We realized the full extent of our misfortune.

※ ※ ※

14   When the weeping ended, I asked the Christians if they would agree to my asking the Indians to take us to their houses. Some of the men who had been in New Spain answered that there was no doubt that if the Indians took us to their houses they would sacrifice us to their idols. But because there was no other solution and the only other path led to certain death, I ignored what these men said. Instead, I begged the Indians to take us to their houses. They showed great pleasure at the idea and told us to wait for a little while and they would do as we wished. Then 30 of them loaded up with firewood and went to their houses, which were quite far away. We stayed with the others until it was almost night.

15   Then they held us closely and quickly set out with us to their houses. Because it was very cold, they were afraid that some of us might die or collapse on the way. So they made four or five large bonfires and placed them at intervals and warmed us at each one. As soon as they saw that we had gotten some strength and warmth they took us to the next fire so quickly that they barely allowed our feet to touch the ground. In this way we went to their houses. There

and in this way we went to their houses, where we found that they had built a house for us with many fires in it; and by an hour after the time we arrived they began to dance and make great revelry (which lasted all night), though for us there was neither pleasure nor revelry nor sleep, waiting to know when they were going to sacrifice us; and next morning they again gave us fish and roots and such good treatment that we felt a little safer and lost to some degree our fear of sacrifice.

16

we found that they had built a house for us with many fires in it.

16   An hour after we arrived they began to dance and have a big party. This lasted all night, though for us there was neither pleasure nor sleep because we were waiting to know when they were going to sacrifice us. But the next morning they again gave us fish and roots and such good treatment that we felt a little safer and lost some of our fear of sacrifice.

from
Of Plymouth Plantation

William Bradford

Safe Arrival at Cape Cod

1   **B**ut to omit other things (that I may be brief) after long beating at sea they fell with that land which is called Cape Cod; the which being made and certainly known to be it, they were not a little joyful. . . .

2   Being thus arrived in a good harbor, and brought safe to land, they fell upon their knees and blessed the God of Heaven who had brought them over the vast and furious ocean, and delivered them from all the perils and miseries thereof, again to set their feet on the firm and stable earth, their proper element. . . .

3   But here I cannot but stay and make a pause, and stand half amazed at this poor people's present condition; and so I think will the reader, too, when he well considers the same. Being thus passed the vast ocean, and a sea of troubles before in their preparation (as may be remembered by that which went

from Of Plymouth Plantation

William Bradford

Safe Arrival at Cape Cod

1   Finally, after a beating at sea, they landed in a place that is called Cape Cod and were filled with joy. . . .

2   After arriving in a good harbor and coming safely to land, they fell on their knees and blessed the God of Heaven who had brought them over the vast, dangerous sea and delivered them from all the dangers and miseries of the trip. Once again they could set their feet on solid ground. . . .

3   But now I must pause and look with amazement at these poor people's situation. I think the reader will be amazed, too, when he stops to think about it. Having just crossed the vast ocean and come through a sea of troubles in preparing for the journey, they now had no friends to welcome them and no inns to

before), they had now no friends to welcome them nor inns to entertain or refresh their weatherbeaten bodies; no houses or much less towns to repair to, to seek for succor. It is recorded in Scripture as a mercy to the Apostle and his shipwrecked company, that the barbarians showed them no small kindness in refreshing them, but these savage barbarians, when they met with them (as after will appear) were readier to fill their sides full of arrows than otherwise.

4   And for the season it was winter, and they that know the winters of that country know them to be sharp and violent, and subject to cruel and fierce storms, dangerous to travel to known places, much more to search an unknown coast. Besides, what could they see but a hideous and desolate wilderness, full of wild beasts and wild men—and what multitudes there might be of them they knew not. Neither could they, as it were, go up to the top of Pisgah to view from this wilderness a more goodly country to feed their hopes; for which way soever they turned their eyes (save upward to the heavens) they could have little solace or content in respect of any outward objects. For summer being done, all things stand upon them with a weatherbeaten face, and the whole country, full of woods and thickets, represented a wild and savage hue. If they looked behind them, there was the mighty ocean which they had passed and was now as a main bar and gulf to separate them from all the civil parts of the world. . . .

5   Being thus arrived at Cape Cod the 11th of November, and necessity calling them to look out a place for habitation (as well as the master's and mariners' importunity); they having brought a large shallop with them out of England, stowed in quarters in the ship, they now got her out and set their carpenters to work to trim her up; but being much

receive and refresh their tired, weatherbeaten bodies. There were no houses, much less towns, to look to for help. The Bible says that the Apostle Paul was greeted courteously by the barbarians after he and his companions were shipwrecked, but the barbarians in this land were ready to fill the new arrivals full of arrows when they first met.

4   In addition, it was winter. Anyone who knows about the winters in that part of the country knows how rough they are and of the fierce storms that make it dangerous to travel to known places, let alone search out an unknown coast. Besides, what could they see but a hideous and lonely wilderness, full of an unknown number of wild beasts and wild men? Nor could they climb to the top of a mountain to see the Promised Land in the distance. Wherever they turned their eyes (except up to the heavens), they found little to comfort them. For summer was over, and everything at this point looked desolate. The whole country, full of woods and thick underbrush, had a wild and rugged appearance. If they looked behind them, there was the mighty ocean which they had crossed and which was now a gulf that separated them from all the civilized parts of the world. . . .

5   They arrived at Cape Cod on the 11th of November and felt the need to look for a place to live, not to mention that the master and the sailors demanded that they do so immediately. They had brought a small open boat with them from England, which they had stowed aboard the ship, and which they now took out and had their carpenters begin

bruised and shattered in the ship with foul weather, they saw she would be long in mending. Whereupon 6 a few of them tendered themselves to go by land and discover those nearest places, whilst the shallop was in mending; and the rather because as they went into that harbor there seemed to be an opening some two or three leagues off, which the master judged to be a river. It was conceived there might be some danger in the attempt, yet seeing them resolute, they were permitted to go, being sixteen of them well armed under the conduct of Captain Standish, having such instructions given them as was thought meet.

7   They set forth the 15th of November; and when they had marched about the space of a mile by the seaside, they espied five or six persons with a dog coming towards them, who were savages; but they fled from them and ran up into the woods, and the English followed them, partly to see if they could

repairing, for the boat had been badly damaged on the ship during the bad weather.

6   When they saw that the boat would take a long time to repair, a few men offered to explore the closest places on the land while the boat was being mended. There seemed to be an opening in the harbor some two or three leagues off which the master thought might be a river. Although there was the possibility of danger, the men were determined to go. Sixteen well-armed men under the command of Captain Standish were permitted to go after receiving proper instructions.

7   They started out the 15th of November, and when they had marched about a mile along the seaside, they spotted five or six savages coming toward them with a dog. The savages fled and ran up into the woods, and the English followed them, partly to see if they could speak with them and partly to see if there

speak with them, and partly to discover if there might not be more of them lying in ambush. But the Indians seeing themselves thus followed, they again forsook the woods and ran away on the sands as hard as they could, so as they could not come near them but followed them by the track of their feet sundry miles and saw that they had come the same way. So, night coming on, they made their rendezvous and set out their sentinels, and rested in quiet that night; and the next

8 morning followed their track till they had headed a great creek and so left the sands, and turned another way into the woods. But they still followed them by guess, hoping to find their dwellings; but they soon lost both them and themselves, falling into such thickets as were ready to tear their clothes and armor in pieces; but were most distressed for want of drink. But at length they found water and refreshed themselves, being the first New England water they drunk of, and was now in great thirst as pleasant unto them as wine or beer had been in foretimes. . . .

9 After this, the shallop being got ready, they set out again for the better discovery of this place, and the master of the ship desired to go himself. So there went some thirty men but found it to be no harbor for ships but only for boats. There was also found two of their houses covered with mats, and sundry of their implements in them, but the people were run away and could not be seen. Also there was found more of their corn and of their beans of various colors; the corn and beans they brought away, purposing to give them full satisfaction when they should meet with any of them as, about some six months afterward they did, to their good content. . . .

10 After some hours' sailing [on the third expedition] it began to snow and rain, and about the middle of the afternoon the wind increased and the sea became

were more lying in ambush. But when the Indians realized they were being followed, they left the woods and ran away on the sands as fast as they could. The English could not get close to the Indians but followed their footprints for several miles and saw that they had come the same way. Then, with night coming, they made camp, set out guards, and rested quietly that night.

8   The next morning they tracked the Indians again until the men had gone around a big creek, left the sand, and turned another way into the woods. They still followed the Indians by guess, hoping to find where they lived, but they soon lost both the Indians and themselves, and fell into thick woods that almost tore off their clothes and armor. The worst part was not having anything to drink, but finally they found water and refreshed themselves with their first New England water. They drank it with as much pleasure as they had drunk wine or beer in the past. . . .

9   After this, the small boat was ready, and the men set out to explore the place better. The master wanted to go with them this time, and about 30 men set out. They soon discovered that this harbor was good for boats but not for ships. They also found two of the savages' houses, covered with mats, with various tools inside, but the people had run away and could not be seen. The English also found more of the Indians' corn and beans of various colors. The English took the corn and beans with the intention of paying for these things if they met any of the Indians, which six months later they did. . . .

10   On the third expedition, after hours of sailing, it began to snow and rain. About the middle of the afternoon the wind increased, and the sea became very

very rough, and they broke their rudder, and it was as much as two men could do to steer her with a couple of oars. But their pilot bade them be of good cheer for he saw the harbor; but the storm increasing, and night drawing on, they bore what sail they could to get in, while they could see. But herewith they broke their mast in three pieces and their sail fell overboard in a very grown sea, so as they had like to have been cast away. Yet by God's mercy they recovered themselves, and having the flood with them,

11 struck into the harbor. But when it came to, the pilot was deceived in the place, and said the Lord be merciful unto them for his eyes never saw that place before; and he and the master's mate would have run her ashore in a cove full of breakers before the wind. But a lusty seaman which steered bade those which rowed, if they were men, about with her or else they were all cast away; the which they did with speed. So he bid them be of good cheer and row lustily, for there was a fair sound before them, and he doubted not but they should find one place or other where

12 they might ride in safety. And though it was very dark and rained sore, yet in the end they got under the lee of a small island and remained there all that night in safety. But they knew not this to be an island till morning, but were divided in their minds; some would keep the boat for fear they might be amongst the Indians, others were so wet and cold they could not endure but got ashore, and with much ado got fire (all things being so wet); and the rest were glad to come to them, for after midnight the wind shifted to the northwest and it froze hard.

13 But though this had been a day and night of much trouble and danger unto them, yet God gave them a morning of comfort and refreshing (as usually

rough. The boat's rudder broke, and it was as much as two men could do to steer the boat with a couple of oars. But their pilot encouraged them to keep going for he saw the harbor. With the storm getting worse and night coming on, they sailed as much as they could while they could see. But then their mast broke in three pieces, and their sail fell overboard in a dangerous sea into which they almost fell themselves. Yet by God's mercy they recovered and having the tide with them, crashed into the waters of the harbor.

11   When they got their bearings, the pilot realized that he had been fooled and asked the Lord to be merciful unto them for his eyes had never seen that place before. He and the master's mate would have run the boat ashore in a small bay full of breaking waves. But a strong sailor who was steering told those who rowed—if they were men—to turn the boat around, or they would all be killed, which they quickly did. Then he told them to buck up and row hard, for there was a wide channel in front of them, and he thought that they would find one place or other where they might ride in safety.

12   Though it was very dark and raining hard, they got under the sheltered side of a small island and stayed safely there all that night. But they did not know this was an island until morning and were divided among themselves. Some wanted to stay on the boat for fear they might be among the Indians. Others were so wet and cold that they could not stay on the boat but went ashore and with great effort got a fire going even though everything was wet. The rest of the men were glad to join them, for after midnight the wind shifted to the northwest, and it froze hard.

13   But even though it had been a day and night of great trouble and danger, God gave them a morning of comfort and new energy, like He usually does to

He doth to His children) for the next day was a fair, sunshining day, and they found themselves to be on an island secure from the Indians, where they might dry their stuff, fix their pieces and rest themselves; and gave God thanks for His mercies in their manifold deliverances. And this being the last day of the week, they prepared there to keep the Sabbath.

14   On Monday they sounded the harbor and found it fit for shipping, and marched into the land and found divers cornfields and little running brooks, a place (as they supposed) fit for situation. At least it was the best they could find, and the season and their present necessity made them glad to accept of it. So they returned to their ship again with this news to the rest of their people, which did much comfort their hearts.

15   On the 15th of December they weighed anchor to go to the place they had discovered, and came within two leagues of it, but were fain to bear up again; but the 16th day, the wind came fair, and they arrived safe in this harbor. And afterwards took better view of the place, and resolved where to pitch their dwelling; and the 25th day began to erect the first house for common use to receive them and their goods.

Compact with the Indians

16   All this while [during January and February 1621] the Indians came skulking about them, and would sometimes show themselves aloof off, but

His children. The next day was fair and sunshiny. They discovered that they were on an island, safe from the Indians, where they might dry their things, fix their guns, and rest. They gave thanks to God for His mercies in their many rescues. And because this was the last day of the week, they prepared to keep the Sabbath the following day.

14   On Monday they measured the depth of the harbor and found it suitable for shipping. They set off into the land, found several cornfields and little running brooks, and a place that they considered fit to inhabit. [Editor's note: This is the Pilgrims' first landing at Plymouth Rock, December 11, 1620.] It was, at least, the best they could find, and because of the time of year and their present needs they were glad to accept it. So they returned to the ship again with this news for the rest of the people, who felt reassured and comforted.

15   On the 15th of December they lifted anchor and went to within two leagues of the place they had discovered but were forced back. On the 16th day the weather turned fair, and they arrived safe in the harbor. [Editor's Note: The *Mayflower* anchored in what was later called Plymouth Harbor on December 16, 1620.] And after taking a good look at the place, they decided where to start building. On the 25th day they began to build the first house for common use to house them and their goods.

Compact with the Indians

16   During January and February of 1621 the Indians lurked around the area and would sometimes appear at a distance. When anyone approached them, they

when any approached near them, they would run away; and once they stole away their tools where they had been at work and were gone to dinner. But about the 16th of March, a certain Indian came boldly amongst them and spoke to them in broken English, which they could well understand but marveled at it. At length they understood by discourse with him, that he was not of these parts, but belonged to the eastern parts where some English ships came to fish, with whom he was acquainted and could name sundry of them by their names, amongst whom he had got his language. He became profitable to them in acquainting them with many things concerning the state of the country in the east parts where he lived, which was afterwards profitable unto them; as also of the people here, of their names, number and strength, of their situation and distance from this place, and who was chief amongst them. His name was Samoset. He told them also of another Indian whose name was Squanto, a native of this place, who had been in England and could speak better English than himself.

17   Being, after some time of entertainment and gifts dismissed, a while after he came again, and five more with him, and they brought again all the tools that were stolen away before, and made way for the coming of their great Sachem, called Massasoit. Who, about four or five days after, came with the chief of his friends and other attendance, with the aforesaid Squanto. With whom, after friendly entertainment and some gifts given him, they made a peace with him (which hath now continued this 24 years) in these terms:

1. That neither he nor any of his should injure or do hurt to any of their people.
2. That if any of his did hurt to any of theirs, he should send the offender, that they might punish him.

would run away. Once the Indians stole the Englishmen's tools while they were at dinner. But about the 16th of March a certain Indian came boldly among the English and spoke to them in broken English which they could understand though it amazed them. Finally, they understood from talking with him that he was not from this area but came from an eastern part of the country. Some English ships had come to fish, and he had gotten acquainted with some of the men and knew a number of them by name, which was how he had learned English. He became useful to them and showed them many helpful things about the eastern part of the country where he lived. His name was Samoset, and he was equally helpful to the people here, telling them the names, number, strength, and distance from this place of the Indians, and name of their chief. Samoset also told the English about another Indian whose name was Squanto, a native of this place who had been in England and could speak better English than Samoset could.

17   After eating, drinking, talking, and receiving gifts, Samoset left, and a while later came back with five others, and they brought all the tools that had been stolen before. They prepared the English for the coming of their great chief, Massasoit. About four or five days later, he came with his most trusted friend, other attendants, and Squanto. After friendly hospitality and gift-giving, the English made a peace with Massasoit (that has continued for 24 years) on these terms:

1. That neither Massasoit nor any of his people would injure or hurt any of the English.
2. That if any of Massasoit's people hurt any of the English, Massasoit would send the offender back to the English for punishment.

3. That if anything were taken away from any of theirs, he should cause it to be restored; and they should do the like to his.

4. If any did unjustly war against him, they would aid him; if any did war against them, he should aid them.

5. He should send to his neighbors confederates to certify them of this, that they might not wrong them, but might be likewise comprised in the conditions of peace.

6. That when their men came to them, they should leave their bows and arrows behind them.

18   After these things he returned to his place called Sowams, some 40 miles from this place, but Squanto continued with them and was their interpreter and was a special instrument sent of God for their good beyond their expectation. He directed them how to set their corn, where to take fish, and to procure other commodities, and was also their pilot to bring them to unknown places for their profit. . . .

19   He was a native of this place, and scarce any [of his tribe were] left alive besides himself. He [had been] carried away with divers others [in 1614] by one Hunt, a master of a ship, who thought to sell them for slaves in Spain. But he got away for England and was entertained by a merchant in London, and employed to Newfoundland and other parts, and lastly brought hither into these parts [in 1618] by one Mr. Dermer, a gentleman employed by Sir Ferdinando Gorges and others for discovery and other designs in these parts. [He learned that his tribe had been destroyed by disease in 1617, so he lived with the settlers at Plymouth] and never left them till he died [in September 1622].

3. That if anything were taken away from any of the English, Massasoit would make sure it was returned, and the English would do the same if any of their people took something from the Indians.

4. If any unjust war were made against Massasoit's people, the English would help the Indians, and if any unjust war were made against the English, the Indians would help the English.

5. That Massasoit would inform his allies about this peace treaty so that they would not hurt the English but might also be part of the peace treaty.

6. That when the Indians came to see the English, the Indians would leave their bows and arrows behind them.

18   After this, Massasoit returned to his place called Sowams, some forty miles away. Squanto, however, stayed with the English and was their interpreter and a special gift from God to help them beyond all their expectations. Squanto showed them how to plant corn, where to fish, and how to get other things they needed. He was also their pilot who brought them to new places that they could profit from.

19   Squanto was a native of this place and hardly any of his tribe were alive besides himself. He had been carried away with many others in 1614 by a man called Hunt, a ship's master, who planned to sell the Indians as slaves in Spain. But Squanto got away to England and was kept as a guest by a merchant in London, and sent to work in Newfoundland and other places. Finally, he was brought to this area in 1618 by a Dr. Denner, a gentleman employed by Sir Ferdinando Gorges and others for exploring and other purposes. Squanto learned that his tribe had been destroyed by disease in 1617, so he lived with the settlers at Plymouth and never left them until he died in September 1622.

To My Dear and Loving Husband

Anne Bradstreet

1   If ever two were one, then surely we.
    If ever man were lov'd by wife, then thee.
    If ever wife was happy in a man,
    Compare with me, ye women, if you can.

2   I prize thy love more than whole Mines of gold
    Or all the riches that the East doth hold.
    My love is such that Rivers cannot quench,
    Nor ought but love from thee give recompetence.

3   Thy love is such I can no
        way repay.
    The heavens reward thee
        manifold, I pray.
    Then while we live, in
        love let's so persever
    That when we live no
        more, we may live
        ever.

The Tenth Muse by Anne Bradstreet, 1650

To My Dear and Loving Husband

Anne Bradstreet

1   If ever two [people] were one, then we are.
If ever a man were loved by a wife, then you are.
If ever a wife was happy with a man—
All you women, compare yourselves with me if you
    can.

2   I value your love more than whole mines of gold
Or all the riches that the East may hold.
My love could not be extinguished by rivers
Nor by anything except your love, freely given.

3   I can never begin to repay you for your love.
I only pray that you will be rewarded by the heavens
    above.
So while we live, let's love by the grace of God ever,
So that even when we die, our love will live forever.

Huswifery

Edward Taylor

1   Make me, O Lord, thy Spinning Wheel complete.
Thy Holy Word my Distaff make for me.
Make mine Affections thy Swift Flyers neat
And make my Soul thy holy Spool to be.
My Conversation make to be thy Reel
And Reel the yarn thereon spun of thy Wheel.

Huswifery

Edward Taylor

To understand this poem you have to understand a little about spinning and weaving, two processes that every self-respecting person in the 17th century knew something about. First, the rough wool or flax was wound around a staff, called a distaff, to prepare it for spinning. Then, the fibers were spun into yarn or thread on a spinning wheel. Next, a weaver crisscrossed the thread or yarn and created cloth on a loom. Edward Taylor, the poet, compares the long process of making a garment at that time to the process by which God purifies human hearts and prepares them for a heavenly existence.

1   In the first verse the speaker compares the process of becoming spiritually perfect to the process of making a wonderful garment. He asks that God's word become the center of his life, like a distaff is the center around which wool is wound. He asks that his feelings be controlled by God, like the "Swift Flyers" control the mechanism of the spinning wheel. He asks that his soul be turned into something new, perfect, and useful like the raw materials that are twisted into thread on a spool. Finally, he asks that his words be wrapped around God, just as thread is wound around a reel, or spool.

2   Make me thy Loom then, knit therein this Twine:
And make thy Holy Spirit, Lord, wind quills.
Then weave the Web thyself. The yarn is fine.
Thine Ordinances make my Fulling Mills.
Then dye the same in Heavenly Colors Choice,
All pinked with Varnished Flowers of Paradise.

3   Then clothe therewith mine Understanding, Will,
Affections, Judgment, Conscience, Memory,
My Words and Actions, that their shine may fill
My ways with glory and thee glorify.
Then mine apparel shall display before ye
That I am Clothed in Holy robes for glory.

Distaff

Spindle

2   In the second verse the speaker asks that God guide all the ins and outs of his life, just as a loom receives the pattern that the weaver weaves upon it. The speaker asks that he be purified by God's laws ("Ordinances"), just as Fulling Mills in the 17th century cleaned, shaped, and shrank wool. The speaker asks God to put the finishing touches of perfection upon him, just as a weaver decides what color to make his garment and how to finish it up.

3   In the last verse, the speaker asks that all of his human characterisitics—his brain, his will, feelings, decision-making, conscience, memory, actions, and words—be perfected to glorify God. He expresses his earnest desire to be wholly perfected and hopes that his life, at its end, will be shown to have glorified God. Then, "Clothed in Holy robes" the speaker will be ready to enter paradise completely purified, perfected, and holy.

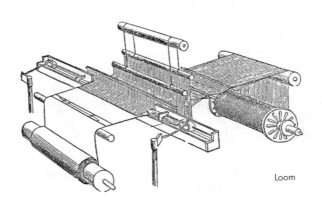

Loom

from Sinners in the Hands of an Angry God

Jonathan Edwards

1   We find it easy to tread on and crush a worm that we see crawling on the earth; so 'tis easy for us to cut or singe a slender thread that any thing hangs by; thus easy is it for God when he pleases to cast his enemies down to Hell. . . .

2   They are now the objects of that very same anger and wrath of God that is expressed in the torments of Hell: and the reason why they don't go down to Hell at each moment, is not because God, in whose power they are, is not then very angry with them; as angry as he is with many of those miserable creatures that he is now tormenting in Hell, and do there feel and bear the fierceness of his wrath. Yea God is a great deal more angry with great numbers that are now on earth, yea doubtless with many that are now in this congregation, that it may be are at ease and quiet, than he is with many of those that are now in the flames of Hell.

3   So that it is not because God is unmindful of their wickedness, and don't resent it, that he don't let loose his hand and cut them off. God is not altogether such an one as themselves, tho' they may imagine him to

from Sinners in the Hands of an Angry God

Jonathan Edwards

1   We find it easy to step on and crush a worm that we see crawling on the earth. It is easy for us to cut or burn a slender thread that an insect hangs on. In the same way it is easy for God, when he pleases, to throw his enemies down into hell. . . .

2   God feels the same anger toward people on earth that he directs at people in hell. The reason that people don't all go to hell right this minute is not because God is not furious with them. God has all the power, and he is very angry with people—as angry as he is at all those miserable creatures that he is already tormenting in hell. Yes indeed, God is a great deal more angry with great numbers of people right here on Earth and with many people sitting right in this congregration than he is with many people who are already in the flames of hell.

3   God does not refrain from cutting down humans because he doesn't know how wicked they are. God is not like humans, though they may imagine him to be. God's wrath burns against humans. Damnation is

be so. The wrath of God burns against them, their damnation don't slumber, the pit is prepared, the fire is made ready, the furnace is now hot, ready to receive them, the flames do now rage and glow. The glittering sword is whet, and held over them, and the pit hath opened her mouth under them. . . .

4   Unconverted men walk over the pit of Hell on a rotten covering, and there are innumerable places in this covering so weak that they won't bear their weight, and these places are not seen. The arrows of death fly unseen at noonday; the sharpest sight can't discern them. God has so many different unsearchable ways of taking wicked men out of the world and sending 'em to Hell, that there is nothing to make it appear that God had need to be at the expense of a miracle, or go out of the ordinary course of his Providence, to destroy any wicked man, at any moment. . . .

5   So that thus it is, that natural men are held in the hand of God over the pit of Hell; they have deserved the fiery pit, and are already sentenced to it; and God is dreadfully provoked, his anger is as great toward them as to those that are actually suffering the executions of the fierceness of his wrath in Hell, and they have done nothing in the least to appease or abate that anger, neither is God in the least bound by any promise to hold 'em up one moment; the Devil is waiting for them, Hell is gaping for them, the flames gather and flash about them, and would fain lay hold on them, and swallow them up; the fire pent up in their own hearts is struggling to break out; and they have no interest in any mediator, there are no means within reach that can be any security to them. In short, they have no refuge, nothing to take hold of, all that preserves them every

waiting, the pit is prepared, the fire has been set, the furnace is hot and ready for humans, and the flames rage and glow. The glitttering sword has been sharpened and is held over these humans. The pit has opened her mouth under them. . . .

4   Men and women who are not saved walk over the pit of hell on a rotten covering. There are many unseen places in this covering that are so weak that they cannot bear people's weight. The arrows of death fly invisibly in the middle of the day. The sharpest eyes cannot see these arrows. God has so many different mysterious ways of taking wicked people out of the world and sending them to hell. It is nothing out of the ordinary for God to destroy any wicked human at any moment. . . .

5   The truth is that humans in their natural, unsaved state are held in the hand of God over the pit of hell. They deserve the fiery pit and are already sentenced to it. God is dreadfully angry. His anger is as great toward these people as it is toward those who are already suffering the horrible pain of his wrath in hell. These people have done nothing to cool down God's anger. Nor has God ever promised to keep people from this fate for even one moment. The Devil is waiting for them. Hell is opening up its mouth to them. The flames gather and blaze about them eager to reach them and swallow them up. The evil fire that is stored up in human hearts is struggling to break out. These people have no interest in someone who can make peace between them and God. There is nothing within reach that can help them. In short, they have no safe place and nothing

moment is the mere arbitrary will, and uncovenanted unobliged forbearance of an incensed God. . . .

6   The bow of God's wrath is bent, and the arrow made ready on the string, and justice bends the arrow at your heart, and strains the bow, and it is nothing but the mere pleasure of God, and that of an angry God, without any promise or obligation at all, that keeps the arrow one moment from being made drunk with your blood.

7   Thus are all you that never passed under a great change of heart, by the mighty power of the spirit of God upon your souls; all that were never born again, and made new creatures, and raised from being dead in sin, to a state of new, and before altogether unexperienced light and life (however you may have reformed your life in many things, and may have had religious affections, and may keep up a form of religion in your families and closets, and in the house of God, and may be strict in it), you are thus in the hands of an angry God; 'tis nothing but his mere pleasure that keeps you from being this moment swallowed up in everlasting destruction. . . .

8   The God that holds you over the pit of Hell, much as one holds a spider, or some loathsome insect, over the fire, abhors you, and is dreadfully provoked; his wrath toward you burns like fire; he looks upon you as worthy of nothing else, but to be cast into the fire; he is of purer eyes than to bear to have you in his sight; you are ten thousand times so abominable in his eyes as the most hateful venomous serpent is in ours. You have offended him infinitely more than ever a stubborn rebel did his prince: and yet 'tis nothing but his hand that holds you from falling into

to take hold of. All that preserves them at any moment is the whim of an angry God who is not obliged in any way to save them. . . .

6   The bow of God's wrath is bent, and the arrow is ready to fly. Justice bends the arrow at your heart and strains the bow. This angry God is not obliged in any way to restrain himself. He may, for whatever reason, decide to let the arrow fly and be made drunk with your blood.

7   This is the condition of you who have not received a great change of heart, by the mighty power of the spirit of God on your souls. This applies to all who have not been born again, made new creatures, raised from being dead in sin, and brought to light and a new life unlike anything you have ever had before. It does not matter what a good person you have made yourself into or how strictly religious you may be with your family, in private, or even in church. You are still in the hands of an angry God. It is nothing but a mere wave of his hand that keeps you from being swallowed up by everlasting destruction at any moment. . . .

8   The God that holds you over the pit of hell, much as one holds a spider or some disgusting insect over a fire, despises you and is dreadfully angry. His wrath toward you burns like fire. He looks upon you as worthy of nothing but to be cast into the fire. His eyes are so pure that he cannot bear to have you in his sight. You are 10,000 times more disgusting in his eyes than the most hated poisonous snake is in our eyes. You have offended God much more than a stubborn rebel ever offended his prince. And yet it is nothing but God's hand that keeps you from falling

the fire every moment: 'tis to be ascribed to nothing else, that you did not go to Hell the last night; that you was suffered to awake again in this world, after you closed your eyes to sleep: and there is no other reason to be given why you have not dropped into Hell since you arose in the morning, but that God's hand has held you up: there is no other reason to be given why you have not gone to Hell since you have sat here in the house of God, provoking his pure eyes by your sinful wicked manner of attending his solemn worship: yea, there is nothing else that is to be given as a reason why you don't this very moment drop down into Hell.

9   O sinner! Consider the fearful danger you are in: 'tis a great furnace of wrath, a wide and bottomless pit, full of the fire of wrath, that you are held over in the hand of that God, whose wrath is provoked and incensed as much against you as against many of the damned in Hell: you hang by a slender thread, with the flames of divine wrath flashing about it, and ready every moment to singe it, and burn it asunder; and you have no interest in any mediator, and nothing to lay hold of to save yourself, nothing to keep off the flames of wrath, nothing of your own, nothing that you ever have done, nothing that you can do, to induce God to spare you one moment. . . .

10   Thus it will be with you that are in an uncon-verted state, if you continue in it; the infinite might, and majesty, and terribleness of the omnipotent God shall be magnified upon you, in the ineffable strength of your torments: you shall be tormented in the presence of the holy angels, and in the presence of the Lamb; and when you shall be in this state of suffering, the glorious inhabitants of Heaven shall go

into the fire every moment. There is no other reason that you did not go to hell last night, that you awoke again this morning, after you closed your eyes to sleep. There is no other reason to be given why you have not dropped into hell since you arose in the morning except that God's hand has held you up. There is no other reason why you have not gone to hell since you have sat here in the house of God, stirring up God's anger by your sinful, wicked way of attending his sacred worship. Yes, there is no other reason why you don't this very moment drop down into hell.

9   O sinner! Think about the fearful danger you are in. It is a great fiery furnace, a wide and bottomless pit, full of the fire of wrath, that you are held over in the hand of that God. His anger is provoked and burns as much against you as against many of the damned in hell. You hang by a slender thread, with the flames of divine wrath blazing about it, and ready every moment to burn and cut the thread. And you have no interest in anyone who can plead your case with God, and there is nothing to lay hold of to save yourself, nothing to keep away the flames of wrath, nothing of your own, that you ever have done, nothing that you can do to convince God to spare you one moment. . . .

10   This is the way it will be with you who have not been saved, if you do nothing different. The great might, majesty, and anger of an all-powerful God will increase the unspeakable torments you experience. You will be tormented in the presence of the holy angels and Jesus. And when you are in this state of suffering, the glorious inhabitants of heaven will go out and look at this awful sight. They will see what

forth and look on the awful spectacle, that they may see what the wrath and fierceness of the Almighty is, and when they have seen it, they will fall down and adore that great power and majesty. . . .

11   . . . 'Tis *everlasting* wrath. It would be dreadful to suffer this fierceness and wrath of Almighty God one moment; but you must suffer it to all eternity: there will be no end to this exquisite horrible misery: when you look forward, you shall see a long forever, a boundless duration before you, which will swallow up your thoughts, and amaze your soul; and you will absolutely despair of ever having any deliverance, any end, any mitigation, any rest at all; you will know certainly that you must wear out long ages, millions of millions of ages, in wrestling and conflict-ing with this almighty merciless vengeance; and then when you have so done, when so many ages have actually been spent by you in this manner, you will know that all is but a point to what remains. So that your punishment will indeed be infinite. Oh, who can express what the state of a soul in such circum-stances is! All that we can possibly say about it, gives but a very feeble faint representation of it; 'tis inex-pressible and inconceivable: for who knows the power of God's anger?

12   How dreadful is the state of those that are daily and hourly in danger of this great wrath, and infinite misery! But this is the dismal case of every soul in this congregation, that has not been born again, how-ever moral and strict, sober and religious they may otherwise be. . . .

13   And now you have an extraordinary opportunity, a day wherein Christ has flung the door of mercy wide open, and stands in the door calling and crying

the anger and power of the Almighty is, and when they have seen it, they will fall down and adore that great power and majesty. . . .

11   . . . It is *everlasting* wrath. It would be dreadful to suffer the rage and terrible anger of Almighty God for one moment, but you will feel it for all eternity. There will be no end to this incredibly horrible misery. When you look forward, you will see a long forever stretched out before you. It will swallow up your thoughts and amaze your soul. You will absolutely despair of ever being rescued or of having any relief, any end, or any rest at all. You will know with an awful certainty that you must spend long ages of time, millions and millions of ages, in conflict with this almighty merciless anger. And then, when you have finished, when many ages have actually gone by in this way, you will know that it is but a tiny pinpoint compared to what lies ahead. So that your punishment will indeed be endless. Oh, who can imagine what a soul in this state will feel! All that we can say cannot even come close. It is impossible to express or imagine, for who knows the power of God's anger?

12   How dreadful is the situation of those who are in daily and hourly danger of this great anger and endless misery! But this is the awful fate of every soul in this congregation who has not been born again, no matter what good people they are or how outwardly religious they are. . . .

13   And now you have an extraordinary opportunity. This day Christ has flung open the door of mercy and stands in the door calling and crying with a loud

14   with a loud voice to poor sinners; a day wherein
      many are flocking to him, and pressing into the king-
      dom of God; many are daily coming from the east,
      west, north, and south; many that were very lately in
      the same miserable condition that you are in, are in
      now an happy state, with their hearts filled with love
      to Him that has loved them and washed them from
      their sins in his own blood, and rejoicing in hope of
      the glory of God. How awful is it to be left behind at
      such a day! To see so many others feasting, while you
      are pining and perishing! To see so many rejoicing
      and singing for joy of heart, while you have cause to
      mourn for sorrow of heart, and howl for vexation of
      spirit! How can you rest one moment in such a
      condition? . . .

15   Therefore let every one that is out of Christ, now
      awake and fly from the wrath to come. . . .

14   voice to poor sinners. Many are flocking to him and coming into the kingdom of God. Many are coming daily from the east, west, north, and south. Many of these people were recently in the same miserable condition that you are in and are now in a happy state. Their hearts are filled with love toward Him who has loved them and washed them from their sins in his own blood. They are rejoicing in hope of the glory of God. How awful to be left behind on such a day! To see so many others feasting, while you are exhausted and dying! To see so many rejoicing and singing with joy while you have reason to mourn and to howl with a troubled spirit. How can you rest one moment in such a condition? . . .

15   Therefore, let everyone that does not belong to Christ, wake up and fly from the judgment that will come. . . .

Unit Two
A New Nation
(1750–1800)

As more and more Europeans arrived in America, they brought with them European thoughts and ideas. The Puritans had preached that humans were basically evil and were saved only by the grace of God. The new ideas coming from Europe said that humans were basically good. What's more, they could use their reason to accomplish just about anything. It was an optimistic, rational view of life. This is why the eighteenth century is called the Age of Reason, or the Enlightenment.

A Reasonable Man

Benjamin Franklin was a man of his time. With a can-do spirit and boundless energy, Franklin thought that anything was possible. He proved it through a life of service and accomplishment. Franklin was an inventor, a statesman, and a writer who believed in common sense, education, and self-improvement.

Revolutionary Voices

Halfway through the century, a crisis began to loom. England, deeply in debt from its latest war with France, called for a series of heavy taxes on the American colonies. The colonists naturally resented the new taxes.

As relations between Britain and America went from bad to worse, American political leaders rose up and began to call for independence. In fact, the crisis leading to the Revolutionary War (1775–1781) produced an astonishing number of brilliant political speakers and writers.

Patrick Henry stirred the hearts of his fellow citizens with speeches that included phrases such as the famous "Give me liberty or give me death!" Thomas Paine, who had been a failure at everything he tried before coming to America, wrote two long pamphlets that became instant best-sellers. His passionate writing helped turn the tide of public opinion against the British. These men spoke and wrote about matters that affected the lives of every colonist. We remember them not only for what they said but for how they said it. Their words are crisp and clear, emotional, rational, and powerful in a way that comes only to those who care deeply about their subjects.

Another leader, Thomas Jefferson, was asked to compose a statement explaining why the 13 colonies were breaking away from the mother country. The result was the Declaration of Independence. This document spells out the basic rights of free men and gives a long list of complaints that led the colonists to finally, reluctantly, declare independence. Millions of schoolchildren have memorized the opening words from that famous document, and freedom fighters around the world continue to be inspired by it.

Citizens and Slaves

Shortly before her husband, John Adams, signed the Declaration of Independence along with 56 others, Abigail Adams wrote the letter that is included in this unit. Though lacking in formal education, Abigail Adams was well read, insightful, and far ahead of her time in the area of women's rights. For ten years, she wrote detailed letters to her husband as he carried out his public duties away from home. Fortunately, these letters were preserved. They reveal both Adams' private life and her opinions about public affairs.

Another letter writer, Frenchman Michel-Guillaume Jean de Crèvecoeur, wrote a series of 12 essays that were published as letters in 1782. Crèvecoeur's most famous letter is included in this unit. It is an optimistic letter because it was an optimistic time. The United States was a new country. She was different from any other country that had ever been. Old prejudices were left behind in Europe, the "Old Country." America was the land of opportunity. Unfortunately, America was not yet a land of opportunity for all. Among the Americans who understood that most keenly were the Africans brought to this country against their will and sold into slavery. Despite the fact that most African slaves had no opportunity for education, a young slave named Phillis Wheatley surprised everyone with her literary poetry. Another African writer, Olaudah Equiano, described the Middle Passage, the horrendous trip from Africa to America, that Equiano and millions of other Africans were forced to take.

Unit Two Author Biographies

Benjamin Franklin
1706–1790

Benjamin Franklin is probably the most widely recognized of the early American writers. His homespun, catchy sayings ("Don't count your chickens until they are hatched") and his *Poor Richard's Almanack* are what many people associate with the name Ben Franklin. But Franklin was much more than a country philosopher. He was a world-respected statesman, publisher, writer, and scientist. His rise from poverty to wealth is an all-American success story. Franklin played a central role in writing the Declaration of Independence and establishing good relations with France, without whose support we might not have won our independence from Britain. Twenty-thousand people attended the funeral of this beloved American. Franklin's *The Autobiography* is considered his masterpiece.

Patrick Henry
1736–1799

Patrick Henry was a fiery speaker who influenced both politicians and ordinary people to support separation from Great Britain. He scolded King George III for the Stamp Act of 1765, which placed a tax on newspapers and other documents produced in the colonies. Ten years later he made the passionate speech to the Virginia convention that is in this unit. His emotional reasoning and skillful use of words brought many who were sitting on the fence over to the side of the revolutionaries. "Give me liberty or give me death!" is one of the most famous quotations in American history. Henry also led the push for adding a Bill of Rights to the U.S. Constitution and later became Governor of Virginia.

Thomas Paine
1737–1809

Thomas Paine's greatest hour came when the country needed him most. Arriving from England in 1774, Paine began writing essays that supported American independence from Britain. On January 10, 1776, Paine published *Common Sense* anonymously. It was the first pamphlet in America to openly propose immediate separation from Britain. It sold half a million copies, a phenomenal number for that day. In December of 1776 he published a series of 16 essays titled *The Crisis* which helped gain more supporters for the cause of independence. During one of the country's darkest hours, Washington read Paine's words to the troops who were about to cross the Delaware River and attack the British at Trenton on Christmas Day.

Abigail Adams
1744–1818

Abigail Adams was the wife of President John Adams and the mother of President John Quincy Adams. She is remembered not only as a wife to one president and a mother to another, but as a woman of influence in her own right. When her husband was away from home for most of a ten-year period helping establish the government of the United States, Abigail Adams kept up a steady stream of correspondence. The letters might have been forgotten had they not been so extraordinary. Abigail Adams' letters show a brilliant mind that was far ahead of its time on the issues of women's rights. Her letters also contain keen observations on the important political figures of the day and on national and international matters facing the new country.

Thomas Jefferson
1743–1826

Thomas Jefferson was the author of the Declaration of Independence. For this reason alone, he would hold a place of honor in American history and literature, but Jefferson achieved much more. He was a statesman, our third president, a talented architect, a brilliant scientist, a fine musician, and an inventor. In addition to the Declaration of Independence, he wrote Virginia's laws on religious freedom. After serving two terms as president, Jefferson retired to Monticello, the Virginia home he had designed for himself. Education was important to Jefferson throughout his life. He founded the University of Virginia and designed both the buildings and the curriculum. He died, fittingly, on the Fourth of July, just 50 years after the Declaration of Independence was adopted.

Phillis Wheatley
c. 1753–1784

Phillis Wheatley was America's first black poet. She came to America as a slave at the age of seven and was purchased by a wealthy tailor under whose roof she received bits of a classical education, an extremely rare occurrence for a slave. Wheatley was a child prodigy, and a poem that she wrote in 1770 made her instantly famous. Her book of poetry, *Poems on Various Subjects*, was published in 1773. For a short period Wheatley was welcomed into literary circles both in America and in England. After a disastrous marriage she disappeared from the limelight and died alone and in poverty.

Michel-Guillaume Jean de Crèvecoeur 1735–1813

Michel-Guillaume Jean de Crèvecoeur was a Frenchman who spent many years in North America as a surveyor and trader. He traveled throughout both Canada and the eastern part of what became the United States. After marrying an American citizen, he became a New York farmer and began writing a series of 12 letters that were eventually titled "Letters from an American Farmer." The letters, published in 1782 in England, attracted a great deal of attention. Europeans were hungry for information about this upstart country that had just won its freedom from Britain. Crèvecoeur's enthusiasm for America helped many people see America as a land where hard work and determination were more important than class and fashion.

Olaudah Equiano 1745–?

Olaudah Equiano was captured as a young boy in the African kingdom of Benin and sold into slavery in Virginia. He was later sold to a Philadelphian who sent him to work in the West Indies. His *Narrative* was first published in London in 1789.

from
The Autobiography

Benjamin Franklin

Moral Perfection

1   *I*t was about this time I conceived the bold and arduous project of arriving at moral perfection. I wished to live without committing any fault at any time; I would conquer all that either natural inclination, custom, or company might lead me into. As I knew, or thought I knew, what was right and wrong, I did not see why I might not always do the one and avoid the other. But I soon found I had undertaken a task of more difficulty than I had imagined. While my care was employed in guarding against one fault, I was often surprised by another; habit took the advantage of inattention; inclination was sometimes too strong for reason. I concluded, at length, that the mere speculative conviction that it was our interest to be completely virtuous was not sufficient to prevent our slipping; and that the contrary habits must be broken, and good ones acquired and established, before we can have any dependence on a steady, uniform rectitude of conduct. For this purpose I therefore contrived the following method.

2   In the various enumerations of the moral virtues I had met within my reading, I found the catalog more or less numerous, as different writers included more or fewer ideas under the same name.

from
The Autobiography

Benjamin Franklin

Moral Perfection

1   *A*round this time I came up with a bold and difficult project—moral perfection. I wanted to live without doing anything wrong at any time. I would conquer everything that either my natural desires, habits, or companions might lead me into. Because I knew, or thought I knew, what was right and wrong, I did not see why I could not always do what was right and avoid what was wrong. But I soon found that I had taken on a task more difficult than I had imagined. When I turned my attention to one fault, I was often surprised by another. Old habits returned when I wasn't paying attention. My natural desires were sometimes too strong for reason. I finally decided that just thinking about being virtuous is not enough to keep us from slipping. Bad habits have to be broken, and good habits have to be acquired and held before we can always behave in a calm, consistent, and honest manner. For this purpose I came up with the following method.

2   In my reading I found that different writers included different ideas under the same moral virtue. Self-restraint, for example, was confined to eating and drinking by some writers. Others expanded its

Temperance, for example, was by some confined to eating and drinking, while by others it was extended to mean the moderating of every other pleasure, appetite, inclination, or passion, bodily or mental, even to our avarice and ambition. I proposed to myself, for the sake of clearness, to use rather more names, with fewer ideas annexed to each, than a few names with more ideas; and I included under thirteen names of virtues all that at that time occurred to me as necessary or desirable, and annexed to each a short precept, which fully expressed the extent I gave to its meaning.

3   These names of virtues, with their precepts, were:

1. TEMPERANCE. Eat not to dullness; drink not to elevation.
2. SILENCE. Speak not but what may benefit others or yourself; avoid trifling conversation.
3. ORDER. Let all your things have their places; let each part of your business have its time.
4. RESOLUTION. Resolve to perform what you ought; perform without fail what you resolve.

5. FRUGALITY. Make no expense but to do good to others or yourself; i.e., waste nothing.
6. INDUSTRY. Lose no time; be always employed in something useful; cut off all unnecessary actions.

7. SINCERITY. Use no hurtful deceit; think innocently and justly, and, if you speak, speak accordingly.
8. JUSTICE. Wrong none by doing injuries, or omitting the benefits that are your duty.

meaning to include every other pleasure, appetite, desire, or passion of body or mind, including greed and ambition. I told myself that for the sake of clarity I would use more terms, with fewer ideas connected to each, rather than a few terms with more ideas. Under 13 virtues I included everything that it seemed good and necessary to include at that time, and I added to each a short maxim which fully expressed the meaning I had in mind.

3   The names of these virtues and their maxims were the following:

1. SELF-RESTRAINT. Do not eat until you feel sluggish. Do not drink to get high.
2. SILENCE. Speak only what may help you or others; avoid small talk.
3. ORDER. Have a place for every thing; plan your work.
4. DETERMINATION. Do what you ought to do. Complete what you have promised to yourself or others.
5. THRIFTINESS. Don't spend money unless it will do you or someone else good. Waste nothing.
6. HARD WORK. Don't waste time. Always be busy doing something useful. Eliminate unnecessary activity.
7. SINCERITY. Do not lie. Think pure and just thoughts. Speak in the same way.
8. JUSTICE. Do not hurt someone by doing wrong or by failing to do the good that is your duty.

4   9. MODERATION. Avoid extremes; forbear resent-
ing injuries so much as you think they deserve.

10. CLEANLINESS. Tolerate no uncleanliness in
body, clothes, or habitation.

11. TRANQUILITY. Be not disturbed at trifles, or at
accidents common or unavoidable.

12. CHASTITY. Rarely use venery but for health
or offspring, never to dullness, weakness, or
the injury of your own or another's peace or
reputation.

13. HUMILITY. Imitate Jesus and Socrates.

5   My intention being to acquire the *habitude* of all
these virtues. I judged it would be well not to distract
my attention by attempting the whole at once, but to
fix it on one of them at a time; and, when I should be
master of that, then to proceed to another, and so on,
till I should have gone through the thirteen; and, as
the previous acquisition of some might facilitate the
acquisition of certain others, I arranged them with
that view, as they stand above. *Temperance* first, as it
tends to procure that coolness and clearness of head
which is so necessary where constant vigilance was
to be kept up, and guard maintained against the
unremitting attraction of ancient habits and the force
of perpetual temptations. This being acquired and
established, *Silence* would be more easy; and my
desire being to gain knowledge at the same time that
I improved in virtue, and considering that in conversation it was obtained rather by the use of the ears
than of the tongue, and therefore wishing to break a
habit I was getting into of prattling, punning, and
joking, which only made me acceptable to trifling
company, I gave *Silence* the second place. This and

4   9. MODERATION. Avoid extremes. Don't hold grudges against those who hurt you even if you think they deserve it.

10. CLEANLINESS. Do not allow yourself, your clothes, or your home to be dirty.

11 PEACEFULNESS. Do not get angry at little things or at simple, unavoidable accidents.

12. PURITY IN SEXUAL MATTERS. Rarely use sex except for health reasons or to conceive children and never to excess or in a way that could damage your own or another person's peace or reputation.

13. HUMILITY. Imitate Jesus and Socrates.

5   I wanted to make *habits* of all of these virtues. I decided that it would be good not to distract my attention by trying to do all of them at once, but to concentrate on them one at a time. When I had mastered one, I would go on to the next and so on, until I had gone through all 13. And because acquiring certain virtues might help me acquire others, I arranged them in the order given above. *Self-restraint* came first, because it leads to a cool and clear head, which helps to guard against old habits and constant temptations. After self-restraint was achieved, it would be easier to attain *Silence*. Along with becoming more virtuous, I wanted to gain more knowledge, and knowledge is obtained more by listening than by speaking. I wanted to break a habit I was getting into of gabbing, joking, and making puns which made me suitable only for unimportant gatherings of people. That was why I gave *Silence* second place. I hoped that *Silence* and the next virtue, *Order*, would give me more time to pay attention to my project and my studies. *Determination*, once it had become a habit, would help me achieve all the remaining virtues. *Thriftiness* and *Hard Work* would

the next, *Order*, I expected would allow me more time for attending to my project and my studies.

Resolution, once become habitual, would keep me firm in my endeavors to obtain all the subsequent virtues; *Frugality* and *Industry* freeing me from my remaining debt, and producing affluence and independence, would make more easy the practice of *Sincerity* and *Justice*, etc., etc. Conceiving then, that, agreeably to the advice of Pythagoras in his Golden Verses, daily examination would be necessary, I contrived the following method for conducting that examination.

6   I made a little book, in which I allotted a page for each of the virtues. I ruled each page with red ink, so as to have seven columns, one for each day of the week, marking each column with a letter for the day. I crossed these columns with thirteen red lines, marking the beginning of each line with the first letter of one of the virtues, on which line, and in its proper column, I might mark, by a little black spot, every fault I found upon examination to have been committed respecting that virtue upon that day.

7   I determined to give a week's strict attention to each of the virtues successively. Thus, in the first week, my great guard was to avoid even the least offence against *Temperance*, leaving the other virtues to their ordinary chance, only marking every evening the faults of the day. Thus, if in the first week I could keep my first line, marked *T*, clear of spots, I supposed the habit of that virtue so much strengthened, and its opposite weakened, that I might venture extending my attention to include the next, and for the following week keep both lines clear of spots. Proceeding thus to the last, I could go through a course complete in thirteen weeks, and four courses in a year. And like him who, having a garden to weed, does not attempt to eradicate all the bad herbs at

free me from my remaining debt and produce wealth and independence. These virtues would make it easier to practice *Sincerity* and *Justice*, etc., etc. Taking the advice of Pythagoras in his Golden Verses, I decided to examine myself daily using the following method.

Poor Richard, 1733.
AN
Almanack
For the Year of Chrift
1733,
Being the Firſt after LEAP YEAR:

And makes ſince the Creation   Years
By the Account of the Eastern *Greeks*   7241
By the Latin Church, when ☉ ent. ♈ .   6932
By the Computation of *W. W.*   5742
By the *Roman* Chronology   5682
By the *Jewiſh* Rabbies   5494

Wherein is contained
The Lunations, Eclipſes, Judgment of the Weather, Spring Tides, Planets Motions & mutual Aſpects, Sun and Moon's Riſing and Setting, Length of Days, Time of High Water, Fairs, Courts, and obſervable Days.
Fitted to the Latitude of Forty Degrees, and a Meridian of Five Hours Weſt from *London*, but may without ſenſible Error, ſerve all the adjacent Places, even from *Newfoundland* to *South-Carolina*.

By *RICHARD SAUNDERS*, Philom.

PHILADELPHIA:
Printed and ſold by *B. FRANKLIN*, at the New Printing-Office near the Market.

Poor Richard's Alamanc

6   I made a little book, in which I allowed a page for each of the virtues. I drew lines on each page with red ink, so that there were seven columns, one for each day of the week, and I marked each column with a letter for the day. I crossed these columns with 13 red lines, marking the beginning of each line with the first letter of one of the virtues. On each line, in its proper column, I made a little black spot for every fault I found after examining myself for that virtue each day.

7   I decided to pay strict attention for a week to each virtue in turn. Thus, in the first week, I tried to avoid doing anything that would go against *Self-restraint*. Every evening I marked the faults of that day in self-restraint, not paying attention to the other virtues. In the first week I hoped I could keep my first line, marked *S*, clear of spots. I thought that if it became a habit to strengthen that virtue and weaken its opposite, I could go further and focus my attention on the next virtue, and the following week could keep both lines clear of spots. I thought I could go along in this way to the end, completing a course in thirteen weeks and four courses in a year. I would be like the gardener who weeds a garden but does not try to get rid of all the bad herbs at once, because that would

once, which would exceed his reach and his strength, but works on one of the beds at a time, and, having accomplished the first, proceeds to a second, so I should have, I hoped, the encouraging pleasure of seeing on my pages the progress I made in virtue, by clearing successively my lines of their spots, till in the end, by a number of courses, I should be happy in viewing a clean book, after a thirteen weeks' daily examination. . . .

8   The precept of *Order* requiring that *every part of my business should have its allotted time,* one page in my little book contained the following scheme of employment for the twenty-four hours of a natural day.

9

THE MORNING. Question: What good shall I do this day?	5 6 7	Rise, wash, and address *Powerful Goodness!* Contrive day's business, and take the resolution of the day; prosecute the present study, and breakfast.
	8 9 10 11	Work.
NOON.	12 1	Read, or overlook my accounts, and dine.
	2 3 4 5	Work.
Question: What good have I done today?	6 7 8 9	Put things in their places. Supper. Music or diversion, or conversation. Examination of the day.
NIGHT.	10 11 12 1 2 3 4	Sleep.

be too hard to do. Instead he works on one of the beds at a time, and when the first is finished moves on to a second. In the same way I hoped to have the great pleasure of seeing my progress in virtue show on my pages. My lines would gradually be cleared of their spots. After a number of courses, I would finally be happy to see, after a 13-week daily examination, a clean book. . . .

8 The maxim of *Order* required that every part of my business should be scheduled. One page in my little book contained the following schedule for one 24-hour day.

9

THE MORNING. Question: What good shall I do this day?	5 6 7	Rise, wash, and address *Powerful Goodness!* Plan the day's work and plan the day's agenda. Carry on with the studies in process and eat breakfast.
	8 9 10 11	Work.
NOON.	12 1	Read or look over my accounts and dine.
	2 3 4 5	Work.
Question: What good have I done today?	6 7 8 9	Put things in their places. Supper. Music or some form of entertainment or conversation. Examination of the day.
NIGHT.	10 11 12 1 2 3 4	Sleep.

from *The Autobiography*

10   I entered upon the execution of this plan for self-examination, and continued it with occasional intermissions for some time. I was surprised to find myself so much fuller of faults than I had imagined; but I had the satisfaction of seeing them diminish. To avoid the trouble of renewing now and then my little book, which, by scraping out the marks on the paper of old faults to make room for new ones in a new course, became full of holes, I transferred my tables and precepts to the ivory leaves of a memorandum book, on which the lines were drawn with red ink, that made a durable stain, and on those lines I marked my faults with a black-lead pencil, which marks I could easily wipe out with a wet sponge. After a while I went through one course only in a year, and afterward only one in several years, till at length I omitted them entirely, being employed in voyages and business abroad, with a multiplicity of affairs that interfered; but I always carried my little book with me. . . .

11   My list of virtues contained at first but twelve; but a Quaker friend having kindly informed me that I was generally thought proud; that my pride showed itself frequently in conversation; that I was not content with being in the right when discussing any point, but was overbearing, and rather insolent, of which he convinced me by mentioning several instances; I determined endeavoring to cure myself, if I could, of this vice or folly among the rest, and I added *Humility* to my list, giving an extensive meaning to the word. . . .

10   I started to execute this plan for self-examination and continued it with occasional interruptions for some time. I was surprised to find that I had more faults than I had imagined, but I had the satisfaction of seeing them decrease. To avoid the trouble of freshening up my little book which became full of holes by scraping out the marks on the paper of old faults to make room for new ones in a new course, I transferred my tables and directions to the ivory pages of a memorandum book. The lines were drawn with permanent red ink and on those lines I marked my faults with a black-lead pencil, whose marks I could easily wipe out with a wet sponge. After a while I went through only one course in a year and then one course in several years. Finally, I stopped doing them completely because I was busy with trips and business abroad and with a great number of other affairs. However, I always carried my little book with me. . . .

11   My list of virtues contained only 12 at first, but a Quaker friend kindly informed me that I was generally thought to be proud. My pride showed itself frequently in conversation. Often I was not content with being right in discussing any point. In fact, I bullied and showed a lack of respect for others, which he convinced me of by mentioning several instances. I was determined to cure myself, if I could, of this fault along with the others, and I added *Humility* to my list, giving a long meaning to the word. . . .

Eating Fish

12   I believe I have omitted mentioning that in my first voyage from Boston, being becalmed off Block Island, our people set about catching cod and hauled up a great many. Hitherto I had stuck to my resolution of not eating animal food; and on this occasion, I considered with my Master Tryon, the taking of every fish as a kind of unprovoked murder, since none of them had or ever could do us any injury that might justify the slaughter. All this seemed very reasonable. But I had formerly been a great lover of fish, and when this came hot out of the frying pan, it smelt admirably well. I balanced some time between principle and inclination till I recollected that when the fish were opened, I saw smaller fish taken out of their stomachs. Then, thought I, if you eat one another, I don't see why we mayn't eat you. So I dined upon cod very heartily and continued to eat with other people, returning only now and then occasionally to a vegetable diet. So convenient a thing it is to be a reasonable creature, since it enables one to find or make a reason for every thing one has a mind to do.

Eating Fish

12   I believe I have not mentioned that in my first trip from Boston, while we were in a calm sea off Block Island, our people set about catching cod and brought in a great haul. Until this time I had stuck to my resolution to not eat animal food. At this time I believed with my Master Tryon that catching fish was a kind of unjustifiable murder, since none of them had or ever could do us any harm that might justify killing them. All this seemed very reasonable. But I had in the past been a great lover of fish, and when they came hot out of the frying pan, they smelled delicious. I went back and forth for a time between my principles and my desires until I remembered that when the fish were cut open, I saw smaller fish taken out of their stomachs. Then, I thought, if you eat one another, I don't see why we can't eat you. So I ate cod with a good appetite and continued to eat them with other people, returning only now and again to a vegetarian diet. It is so convenient to be a reasonable person, since it allows one to find or make a reason for everything one wants to do.

Speech in the Virginia Convention

Patrick Henry

March 23, 1775

1   *M*r. President: No man thinks more highly than I do of the patriotism, as well as abilities, of the very worthy gentlemen who have just addressed the house. But different men often see the same subject in different lights; and, therefore, I hope it will not be thought disrespectful to those gentlemen, if, entertaining, as I do, opinions of a character very opposite to theirs, I shall speak forth my sentiments freely and without reserve. This is no time for ceremony. The question before the house is one of awful moment to this country. For my own part, I consider it as nothing less than a question of freedom or slavery. And in proportion to the magnitude of the subject ought to be the freedom of the debate. It is only in this way that we can hope to arrive at truth, and fulfill the great responsibility which we hold to God and our country. Should I keep back my opinions at such a time, through fear of giving offense, I should consider myself as guilty of treason toward my country, and of an act of disloyalty toward the Majesty of Heaven, which I revere above all earthly kings.

Speech in the Virginia Convention

Patrick Henry

March 23, 1775

1   *M*r. President: I do not question the patriotism or the abilities of the gentlemen who have just spoken. Different men see things differently, and I hope no one will think that I am disrespectful by presenting an opposing viewpoint. I will speak from the heart and hold nothing back because this is no time for pretense. The question before the house is of the utmost importance. We are talking about being slaves or being free men.

Because this is such an important subject, we must examine it from every angle. Only in this way can we find the truth and fulfill the responsibilities we have to God and country. If I held back my true feelings at such a time, out of fear of offending someone, I would be guilty of treason against my country and against the Almighty, whom I honor above all earthly rulers.

2   Mr. President, it is natural to man to indulge in the illusions of hope. We are apt to shut our eyes against a painful truth, and listen to the song of that siren till she transforms us into beasts. Is this the part of wise men, engaged in a great and arduous struggle for liberty? Are we disposed to be of the number of those who having eyes see not, and having ears hear not, the things which so nearly concern their temporal salvation? For my part, whatever anguish of spirit it may cost, I am willing to know the whole truth; to know the worst and to provide for it.

3   I have but one lamp by which my feet are guided, and that is the lamp of experience. I know of no way of judging of the future but by the past. And judging by the past, I wish to know what there has been in the conduct of the British ministry for the last ten years to justify those hopes with which gentlemen have been pleased to solace themselves and the house? Is it that insidious smile with which our petition has been lately received? Trust it not, sir; it will prove a snare to your feet. Suffer not yourselves to be betrayed with a kiss. Ask yourselves how this gracious reception of our petition comports with those warlike preparations which cover our waters and darken our land. Are fleets and armies necessary to a work of love and reconciliation? Have we shown ourselves so unwilling to be reconciled that force must be called in to win back our love? Let us not deceive ourselves, sir. These are the implements of war and subjugation—the last arguments to which kings resort.

4   I ask gentlemen, sir, what means this martial array, if its purpose be not to force us to submission? Can gentlemen assign any other possible motive for it? Has Great Britain any enemy in this quarter of

2   Mr. President, it is natural to hang onto false hope. Men often close their eyes to painful truths and let themselves be lulled by sirens[1] who turn them into beasts. Is this what wise men who are in a great fight for liberty should do? Should we be like the people in the Hebrew Scriptures who had eyes but did not see and ears but did not hear what they needed to hear to save themselves? I, for one, would rather know the whole truth, awful as it may be, so that I might be prepared.

3   I can only judge by experience. I don't know of any other way to guess the future except by the past. And judging by the past, I'd like to know what in Britain's actions over the last 10 years could give anyone the kind of hope that the former speakers expressed. Was it the deceitful smile that greeted our last petition? Don't trust it for a minute, or you will be lost. Don't let yourself be betrayed with a kiss as Judas was. Ask yourself how this "gracious" act fits with the preparations for war which we see at land and at sea. Do armies and navies work for peace? Have we been so difficult that they must call out their armies to show us they love us? Let us not fool ourselves, sir. These are the tools of control and war—the last arguments that kings use.

4   I ask the gentlemen here, what is the purpose of this military presence if not to bring us to our knees? Can gentlemen think of any other possible reason? Does Great Britain have any other enemy in this

1 **sirens:** This is an allusion to Homer's *Odyssey* in which sirens, who were half women, half birds, lured sailers to their deaths.

the world, to call for all this accumulation of navies and armies? No, sir, she has none. They are meant for us: they can be meant for no other. They are sent over to bind and rivet upon us those chains which the British ministry have been so long forging.

5   And what have we to oppose to them? Shall we try argument? Sir, we have been trying that for the last ten years. Have we anything new to offer upon the subject? Nothing. We have held the subject up in every light of which it is capable; but it has been all in vain. Shall we resort to entreaty and humble supplication? What terms shall we find which have not been already exhausted? Let us not, I beseech you, sir, deceive ourselves longer.

6   Sir, we have done everything that could be done to avert the storm which is now coming on. We have petitioned; we have remonstrated; we have supplicated; we have prostrated ourselves before the throne, and have implored its interposition to arrest the tyrannical hands of the ministry and Parliament. Our petitions have been slighted; our remonstrances have produced additional violence and insult; our supplications have been disregarded; and we have been spurned with contempt from the foot of the throne! In vain, after these things, may we indulge the fond hope of peace and reconciliation. There is no longer any room for hope. If we wish to be free, if we mean to preserve inviolate those inestimable privileges for which we have been so long contending, if we mean not basely to abandon the noble struggle in which we have been so long engaged, and which we have pledged ourselves never to abandon until the glorious object of our contest shall be obtained—we must fight! I repeat it, sir, we must fight! An appeal to arms and to the God of Hosts is all that is left us!

part of the world that would explain why these armies and navies are here? No, she does not. They are meant for us. There is no other explanation. They are sent to enslave us in the way that Britain has been trying to do for a long time.

5   And how can we oppose them? Shall we try reason? Sir, we have tried reason for the past ten years. Is there anything new to say on the subject? No. We have tried to talk about the subject from every angle, but it has done no good. Shall we try begging our cause? What can we do that has not already been done? Let us not fool ourselves any longer.

6   Sir, we have done everything possible to avoid the storm that is brewing. We have written petitions, we have protested, we have pleaded, we have thrown ourselves before the king and begged him to stop the injustice of the ministry and Parliament. Our petitions have been overlooked, our protests have only brought violent reactions, and our pleas have been set aside. We have been rejected and scorned by the king. After all this we still hoped for a peaceful settlement. Hope is now useless. If we wish to be free, if we wish to preserve the principles that we believe in, if we do not want to give up all that we have struggled and worked for—and which we have promised ourselves never to give up until we are successful—we must fight! I say it again, sir. We must fight! A call to fight and a plea to our God is all that is left!

7   They tell us, sir, that we are weak—unable to cope with so formidable an adversary. But when shall we be stronger? Will it be the next week, or the next year? Will it be when we are totally disarmed, and when a British guard shall be stationed in every house? Shall we gather strength by irresolution and inaction? Shall we acquire the means of effectual resistance by lying supinely on our backs and hugging the delusive phantom of hope until our enemies shall have bound us hand and foot? Sir, we are not weak, if we make a proper use of those means which the God of nature hath placed in our power. Three millions of people, armed in the holy cause of liberty, and in such a country as that which we possess, are invincible by any force which our enemy can send against us. Besides, sir, we shall not fight our battles alone. There is a just God who presides over the destinies of nations and who will raise up friends to fight our battles for us. The battle, sir, is not to the strong alone; it is to the vigilant, the active, the brave. Besides, sir, we have no election. If we were base enough to desire it, it is now too late to retire from the contest. There is no retreat but in submission and slavery! Our chains are forged! Their clanging may be heard on the plains of Boston! The war is inevitable—and let it come! I repeat it, sir, let it come!

8   It is in vain, sir, to extenuate the matter. Gentlemen may cry, "Peace, peace"—but there is no peace. The war is actually begun! The next gale that sweeps from the north will bring to our ears the clash of resounding arms! Our brethren are already in the field! Why stand we here idle? What is it that gentlemen wish? What would they have? Is life so dear, or peace so sweet, as to be purchased at the price of chains and slavery? Forbid it, Almighty God! I know not what course others may take; but as for me, give me liberty or give me death!

7   They say, sir, that we are weak, that we will be unable to fight such a strong enemy. But when will we be stronger? Next week? Next year? Should we wait until the British have disarmed us and posted a guard at every house? Shall we gather strength by doing nothing? Shall we equip ourselves for battle by lying on our backs and hoping everything will go away, until our enemies have taken total control? Sir, we are not weak if we use what God has given us. Three million armed people in this country who believe in a Holy Cause cannot be defeated. Besides, we will not be alone. A just God who cares about the nations will recruit allies for us. Strength is not the only thing that counts. The battle will be won by those who are alert, active, and brave. Besides, sir, we have no choice. There is no turning back, except to give in and be slaves! Our chains have already been made. You can hear them clanging on the plains of Boston! The war cannot be stopped. Let it come! I repeat, sir, let it come!

8   It does no good to drag things out. Gentlemen may cry, "Peace, peace," but there is no peace. The war has actually begun. The next wind from the north will bring the sound of armies at war. Our brothers are already in the field! Why are we standing around doing nothing? What do the gentlemen want? Is life so precious, or peace so sweet, as to be bought at any price, even chains and slavery? Dear God, don't allow it! I do not know what choice others may make, but as for me, give me liberty or give me death!

from The Crisis

Thomas Paine

1   These are the times that try men's souls. The summer soldier and the sunshine patriot will, in this crisis, shrink from the service of their country; but he that stands it *now* deserves the love and thanks of man and woman. Tyranny, like hell, is not easily conquered; yet we have this consolation with us, that the harder the conflict, the more glorious the triumph. What we obtain too cheap, we esteem too lightly; it is dearness only that gives everything its value. Heaven knows how to put a proper price upon its goods, and it would be strange indeed if so celestial an article as *freedom* should not be highly rated. Britain, with an army to enforce her tyranny, had declared that she has a right not only to *tax*, but "to *bind* us in *all cases whatsoever*"; and if being *bound in that manner* is not slavery, then is there not such a thing as slavery upon earth. Even the expression is impious, for so unlimited a power can belong only to God. . . .

2   I have as little superstition in me as any man living, but my secret opinion has ever been, and still is, that God Almighty will not give up a people to military destruction, or leave them unsupportedly to perish, who have so earnestly and so repeatedly sought to avoid the calamities of war, by every decent method which wisdom could invent. Neither have I so much of the infidel in me as to suppose that He

from The Crisis

Thomas Paine

1   These are the most difficult of times. Our fair-weather friends are nowhere to be seen during this crisis in their country, but those who stand firm deserve our love and thanks. A cruel and unjust government is as hard to overthrow as it would be to overthrow hell. But we have this promise: the more difficult the fight, the more glorious will be the victory. If we receive something too easily, we don't appreciate it; we value what comes at a high cost. Only heaven knows what is really important, and certainly it would be strange if heaven did not value *freedom* above all else. Britain, with an army to back up her unjust laws, says that she has a right to pass whatever laws she chooses, as well as to tax us. If accepting any law that Britain lays on us is not slavery, then what is? Allowing any government to have that kind of power is against the will of God, who alone has unlimited power.

2   Now I am not a superstitious man, but in my heart I believe that God will not desert or allow an army to destroy a people who have tried to avoid the horrors of war, by every means possible. Neither am I such a skeptic that I believe God has stopped ruling the world and has left devils in charge. I do not see how the king of Britain can ask God for help. A murderer or a robber has as good a claim to God's help as the king of Britain has. . . .

has relinquished the government of the world, and given us up to the care of devils; and as I do not, I cannot see on what grounds the king of Britain can look up to heaven for help against us: a common murderer, a highwayman, or a housebreaker has as good a pretense as he. . . .

3   I once felt all that kind of anger which a man ought to feel against the mean principles that are held by the Tories. A noted one, who kept a tavern at Amboy, was standing at his door, with as pretty a child in his hand, about eight or nine years old, as ever I saw, and after speaking his mind as freely as he thought was prudent, finished with this unfatherly expression, "Well, give me peace in my day." Not a man lives on the continent, but fully believes that a separation must sometime or other finally take place, and a generous parent should have said, "If there must be trouble, let it be in my day, that my child may have peace"; and this single reflection, well applied, is sufficient to awaken every man to duty. Not a place upon earth might be so happy as America. Her situation is remote from all the wrangling world, and she has nothing to do but trade with them. A man can distinguish himself between temper and principle, and I am as confident as I am that God governs the world, that America will never be happy till she gets clear of foreign dominion. Wars, without ceasing, will break out till that period arrives, and the continent must in the end be conqueror; for though the flame of liberty may sometimes cease to shine, the coal can never expire. . . .

4   The heart that feels not now is dead; the blood of his children will curse his cowardice who shrinks back at a time when a little might have saved the whole, and made *them* happy. I love the man that can smile in trouble, that can gather strength from distress, and grow

3   I once felt great anger toward the selfish principles of the Tories.[1] One of these fellows had a tavern at Amboy, New Jersey. He stood by the door holding the hand of a sweet-looking child about eight or nine years old. After he had finished speaking his mind freely, he said something that wasn't fatherly at all. "Let me live my life in peace!" he said. There is no one on this continent who does not believe that Britain and America must eventually separate. A good parent would have said, "If there has to be trouble, let it come now, so that my child may live in peace." Giving this incident careful thought should convince every man of his duty. America could be the happiest place on earth. She is far away from the problems in other countries; all she has to do is trade with them. A man must figure out where he stands, but as sure as God rules the earth, I believe that America will not be happy until she is free of foreign rule. Wars will keep breaking out until we rule our continent. Though the light of freedom burns dimly at times, it can never be put out entirely. . . .

4   Anyone whose heart is not moved by what is happening now must be dead. If men do not step up when a little effort could change everything for the better, future generations will curse them as

1 **Tories:** supporters of Great Britain

brave by reflection. 'Tis the business of little minds to shrink; but he whose heart is firm, and whose conscience approves his conduct, will pursue his principles unto death. My own line of reasoning is to myself as straight and clear as a ray of light. Not all the treasures of the world, so far as I believe, could have induced me to support an offensive war, for I think it murder; but if a thief breaks into my house, burns and destroys my property, and kills or threatens to kill me, or those that are in it, and to "bind me in all cases whatsoever" to his absolute will, am I to suffer it? What signifies it to me whether he who does it is a king or a common man; my countryman or not my countryman; whether it be done by an individual villain, or any army of them? If we reason to the root of things we shall find no difference; neither can any just cause be assigned why we should punish in the one case and pardon in the other.

cowards. I love the man who smiles at trouble and lets it make him stronger and braver. Little minds wither with trouble, but the person with a good, clear conscience will follow his principles unto death. My thinking on this matter seems to me as straight and clear as a ray of light. Not all the riches in the world could have convinced me to take the offensive in war; I consider that murder. But if a robber breaks into and enters my home, burns and destroys my property, threatens to kill me or my family, and tells me I must do whatever he tells me to do, am I supposed to just take it? What difference does it make whether the one who does it is a king or a commoner, my neighbor or a foreigner? Does it matter if it is done by one person or a whole army? If we really think about this, we will see that there is no difference. There is no reason why we should go after the culprit in one case and excuse the abuse in the other.

Washington prepares to cross the Delaware with 2,400 men.

Letter to
Her Husband

Abigail Adams

Braintree
May 7, 1776

1 *H*ow many are the solitary hours I spend,
ruminating upon the past and anticipating
the future whilst you, overwhelmed with
the cares of state, have but few moments you can
devote to any individual. All domestic pleasures and
enjoyments are absorbed in the great and important
duty you owe your country "for our country is, as it
were, a secondary god and the first and greatest parent. It is to be preferred to parents, wives, children,
friends and all things; the gods only excepted. For if
our country perishes, it is as impossible to save an
individual as to preserve one of the fingers of a mor-
tified hand." Thus do I suppress every wish and
silence every murmur, acquiescing in a painful separation of my youth and the friend of my heart.

2 I believe it is near ten days since I wrote you a
line. I have not felt in a humor to entertain you. If I
had taken up my pen, perhaps some unbecoming
invective might have fallen from it; the eyes of our
rulers have been closed and a lethargy has seized

Letter to
Her Husband

Abigail Adams

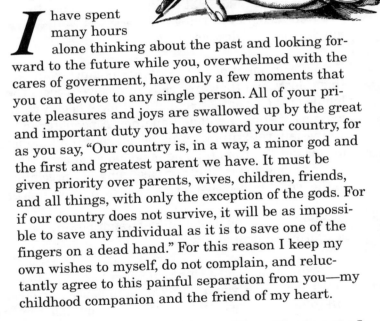

Braintree
May 7, 1776

1   *I* have spent many hours alone thinking about the past and looking forward to the future while you, overwhelmed with the cares of government, have only a few moments that you can devote to any single person. All of your private pleasures and joys are swallowed up by the great and important duty you have toward your country, for as you say, "Our country is, in a way, a minor god and the first and greatest parent we have. It must be given priority over parents, wives, children, friends, and all things, with only the exception of the gods. For if our country does not survive, it will be as impossible to save any individual as it is to save one of the fingers on a dead hand." For this reason I keep my own wishes to myself, do not complain, and reluctantly agree to this painful separation from you—my childhood companion and the friend of my heart.

2   I believe it is almost ten days since I last wrote. I have not been in the right mood to write. If I had, I might have written some harshly critical words that would put me in a bad light. Our rulers' eyes have been closed, and a spirit of indifference has come

almost every member. I fear a fatal security has taken possession of them. Whilst the building is in flame, they tremble at the expense of water to quench it. In short, two months have elapsed since the evacuation of Boston, and very little has been done in that time to secure it or the harbor from future invasion until the people are all in a flame, and no one among us that I have heard of even mentions expense. They think universally that there has been an amazing neglect somewhere. Many have turned out as volunteers to work upon Nodles Island, and many more would go upon Nantasket if it was once set on foot. "It is a maxim of state that power and liberty are like heat and moisture; where they are well mixed everything prospers; where they are single, they are destructive."

3   A government of more stability is much wanted in this colony, and they are ready to receive it from the hands of the Congress, and since I have begun with maxims of state, I will add another: A people may let a king fall, yet still remain a people, but if a king lets his people slip from him, he is no longer a king. And as this is most certainly our case, why not proclaim to the world in decisive terms your own importance?

4   Shall we not be despised by foreign powers for hesitating so long at a word?

5   I cannot say that I think you very generous to the ladies, for whilst you are proclaiming peace and good will to men, emancipating all nations, you insist upon retaining an absolute power over wives. But you must remember that arbitrary power is like most other things which are very hard, very liable to be broken—and notwithstanding all your wise laws and maxims, we have it in our power not only to free our-

over almost everyone. I am afraid that a sense of false security has taken hold of them. While the building is on fire, they are afraid to spend money on water to put it out. In short, two months have passed since the evacuation of Boston, and very little has been done in that time to protect the city or the harbor from future invasion until they are all on fire. No one that I know of even thinks of what it would cost. They all think that there has been gross neglect somewhere. Many have become volunteers on Nodles Island, and many more would go to Nantasket if they could. "It is widely believed in government that power and liberty are like heat and water. When they are mixed well everything grows, but when they are by themselves, they are destructive."

3   People in this colony want a more stable government, and they are ready to receive it from the hands of Congress. Since I began with some truths about government, I will add yet another: A people may let a king fall, yet still remain a people, but if a king lets his people slip away from him, he is no longer a king. And since this is most certainly our case, why not tell the world in no uncertain terms where you stand?

4   Will we not be looked down upon by foreign governments for waiting so long to speak?

5   I do not think you are very generous to the ladies, for while you are proclaiming peace and good will to men and freeing all nations, you insist upon holding absolute power over wives. But you must remember that absolute power is like most other things that are very hard. It is very likely to be broken. Even with all your wise laws and great truths, we have it in our power not only to free ourselves but to bring down

selves but to subdue our masters, and with out violence throw both your natural and legal authority at
our feet—

6   Charm by accepting, by submitting sway
        Yet have our humor most when we obey.

7   I thank you for several letters which I have
received since I wrote last. They alleviate a tedious
absence, and I long earnestly for a Saturday evening
and experience a similar pleasure to that which I
used to find in the return of my friend upon that day
after a week's absence. The idea of a year dissolves
all my philosophy.

8   Our little ones, whom you so often recommend to
my care and instruction, shall not be deficient in
virtue or probity if the precepts of a mother have
their desired effect, but they would be doubly
enforced could they be indulged with the example of
a father constantly before them; I often point them to
their sire

9   Engaged in a corrupted state
        Wrestling with vice and faction.

our masters without violence and to throw both your natural and legal authority at our feet—

6   We charm men through approval and giving in
     Yet please most when we obey.

7   Thank you for the letters which I received since I last wrote. They help me to survive the difficult time apart, but I long for a Saturday evening and the pleasure I used to have at seeing my friend return after a week's absence. The idea of a year apart is hard to imagine.

8   Our children, whom you have put in my care and asked me to teach, will not lack goodness and honesty if I have anything to do about it, but they would learn their lessons twice as well if their father were present to set an example for them. I often point them to their respected father

9   Busy with the dirty business of government
     Fighting evil and quarreling.

The Declaration of Independence

Thomas Jefferson

1   When in the Course of human events, it becomes necessary for one people to dissolve the political bands which have connected them with another, and to assume among the powers of the earth, the separate and equal station to which the Laws of Nature and of Nature's God entitle them, a decent respect to the opinions of mankind requires that they should declare the causes which impel them to the separation.

2   We hold these truths to be self-evident, that all men are created equal, that they are endowed by their Creator with certain unalienable Rights, that among these are Life, Liberty and the pursuit of Happiness.—That to secure these rights, Governments are instituted among Men, deriving their just powers from the consent of the governed, —That whenever any Form of Government becomes destructive of these ends, it is the Right of the People to alter or to abolish it, and to institute new Government, laying its foundation on such principles and organizing its powers in such form, as to them shall seem most likely to effect their Safety and Happiness. Prudence, indeed, will dictate that

The Declaration of Independence

Thomas Jefferson

1   Sometimes it becomes necessary for one people to break the political bonds that have connected them to another. Under the laws of God and nature they must take their place, separate and equal, among the powers of the earth. Out of respect for world opinion they need to explain what moved them toward separation.

2   We believe that certain truths are obvious. All men are created equal. Their Creator has given them certain rights that cannot be taken away. These include their right to live, to be free, and to pursue their dreams for happiness. To guarantee these rights, governments are set up that receive their power from the people they serve. When a government does not respect these ideals, the people have a right to change the government, or to do away with it. They may set up a new government that is based on their ideals and on an organization of power that is most likely to produce safety and happiness for the people. Common sense tells us that a government that has been around for a long time should not be

Governments long established should not be changed for light and transient causes; and accordingly all experience hath shown, that mankind are more disposed to suffer, while evils are sufferable, than to right themselves by abolishing the forms to which they are accustomed. But when a long train of abuses and usurpations, pursuing invariably the same Object evinces a design to reduce them under absolute Despotism, it is their right, it is their duty, to throw off such Government, and to provide new Guards for their future security.

3   Such has been the patient sufferance of these Colonies; and such is now the necessity which constrains them to alter their former Systems of Government. The history of the present King of Great Britain is a history of repeated injuries and usurpations, all having in direct object the establishment of an absolute Tyranny over these States. To prove this, let Facts be submitted to a candid world.

4   He has refused his Assent to Laws, the most wholesome and necessary for the public good.

5   He has forbidden his Governors to pass Laws of immediate and pressing importance, unless suspended in their operation till his Assent should be obtained; and when so suspended, he has utterly neglected to attend to them.

6   He has refused to pass other Laws for the accommodation of large districts of people, unless those people would relinquish the right of Representation in the Legislature, a right inestimable to them and formidable to tyrants only.

changed for trivial reasons. In fact, people will usually put up with things they have grown used to (rather than change them) as long as the evil is not too great. But when a long list of abuses of power shows a pattern of tyranny, it is the right and the duty of the people to put an end to this kind of government and to find new ways to protect their future security.

3   These colonies have patiently endured abuses, but it is now necessary for them to change their system of government. The history of the present king of Great Britain is a history of repeated injuries and unlawful seizures of power. His purpose is to establish an absolute tyranny over these states. To prove this, the following facts are presented to the world.

4   He has refused to agree to laws that are beneficial and necessary for the public good.

5   He has forbidden his governors to pass laws that are urgently needed unless all action is stopped while his approval is obtained. But when a law is held up in this way, he completely neglects to pay any attention to the matter.

6   He has refused to pass other laws for the benefit of large districts of people unless those people give up the right of representation in the legislature. This right has the greatest value to the people and is a threat only to tyrants.

7   He has called together legislative bodies at places unusual, uncomfortable, and distant from the depository of their public Records, for the sole purpose of fatiguing them into compliance with his measures.

8   He has dissolved Representative Houses repeatedly, for opposing with manly firmness his invasions on the rights of the people.

9   He has refused for a long time, after such dissolutions, to cause others to be elected; whereby the Legislative powers, incapable of Annihilation, have returned to the People at large for their exercise; the State remaining in the mean time exposed to all the dangers of invasion from without, and convulsions within.

10   He has endeavoured to prevent the population of these States; for that purpose obstructing the Laws for Naturalization of Foreigners; refusing to pass others to encourage their migrations hither, and raising the conditions of new Appropriations of Lands.

11   He has obstructed the Administration of Justice, by refusing his Assent to Laws for establishing Judiciary powers.

12   He has made Judges dependent on his Will alone, for the tenure of their offices, and the amount and payment of their salaries.

13   He has erected a multitude of New Offices, and sent hither swarms of Officers to harrass our people, and eat out their substance.

14   He has kept among us, in times of peace, Standing Armies without the Consent of our legislatures.

7   He has made the legislature meet at unusual and odd places far away from their offices for the sole purpose of wearing out the legislators and getting them to go along with his actions.

8   He has repeatedly broken up Houses of Representatives because they had the courage to oppose his attempts to take away the people's rights.

9   He has refused to allow new legislatures to be elected long after breaking up the old ones. The legislative power, therefore, returns to the people, since it cannot be destroyed. The state, in the meantime, is exposed to the dangers of attack from the outside and to violent disturbances from within.

10   He has tried to prevent additional people from populating these states. For that reason he has blocked laws that would let foreigners become citizens. He refuses to pass other laws that would encourage emigration to this country, and he has made it difficult to acquire new territory.

11   He has blocked justice by refusing to agree to laws that would establish courts of law.

12   He has made judges dependent on his will alone, for their term of office and the amount and payment of their salaries.

13   He has set up a great many new offices and sent out many officers to torment our people and make their lives difficult.

14   He has kept standing armies among us in peace time without the consent of our legislature.

15 He has affected to render the Military independent of and superior to the Civil power.

16 He has combined with others to subject us to a jurisdiction foreign to our constitution, and unacknowledged by our laws; giving his Assent to their Acts of pretended Legislation:

17 For Quartering large bodies of armed troops among us:

18 For protecting them, by a mock Trial, from punishment for any Murders which they should commit on the Inhabitants of these States:

19 For cutting off our Trade with all parts of the world:

20 For imposing Taxes on us without our Consent:

21 For depriving us in many cases, of the benefits of Trial by Jury:

22 For transporting us beyond Seas to be tried for pretended offences:

23 For abolishing the free System of English Laws in a neighbouring Province, establishing therein an Arbitrary government, and enlarging its Boundaries so as to render it at once an example and fit instrument for introducing the same absolute rule into these Colonies:

24 For taking away our Charters, abolishing our most valuable Laws, and altering fundamentally the Forms of our Governments:

15   He has tried to make the military independent of, and superior to, civil power.

16   He has joined with others to impose laws that go against our constitution. These so-called laws give his permisssion for the following:

17   To force us to house large numbers of soldiers among us.

18   To protect these soldiers, by mock trials, from punishment for any murders of our people that they commit.

19   To cut off our trade with all parts of the world.

20   To tax us without our consent.

21   To deprive us in many cases of the benefit of trial by jury.

22   To bring us overseas for trial on made-up crimes.

23   To do away with the free system of English laws in a neighboring province and to set up a dictatorship. To expand this type of government as an example to the people and to use it to introduce absolute rule into these colonies.

24   To take away the documents by which we originally organized ourselves, do away with our most valuable laws, and to fundamentally change the forms of our governments.

25   For suspending our own Legislatures, and declaring themselves invested with power to legislate for us in all cases whatsoever.

26   He has abdicated Government here, by declaring us out of his Protection and waging War against us.

27   He has plundered our seas, ravaged our Coasts, burnt our towns, and destroyed the lives of our people.

28   He is at this time transporting large Armies of foreign Mercenaries to complete the works of death, desolation and tyranny, already begun with circumstances of Cruelty & perfidy scarcely paralleled in the most barbarous ages, and totally unworthy the Head of a civilized nation.

29   He has constrained our fellow Citizens taken Captive on the high Seas to bear Arms against their Country, to become the executioners of their friends and Brethren, or to fall themselves by their Hands.

30   He has excited domestic insurrections amongst us, and has endeavoured to bring on the inhabitants of our frontiers, the merciless Indian Savages, whose known rule of warfare, is an undistinguished destruction of all ages, sexes and conditions.

31   In every stage of these Oppressions We have Petitioned for Redress in the most humble terms: Our repeated Petitions have been answered only by repeated injury. A Prince whose character is thus marked by every act which may define a Tyrant, is unfit to be the ruler of a free people.

32   Nor have We been wanting in attentions to our British brethren.

25   To stop our legislatures from functioning and to declare themselves as having legislative power over us in all cases.

26   He has given up his authority by stating that we are no longer under his protection and that he is waging war against us.

27   He has looted our seas, ruined our coasts, burned our towns, and destroyed our people's lives.

28   He is currently sending large armies of foreign soldiers to complete the works of death, destruction, and tyranny that began with acts of cruelty and betrayal almost unparalled in the most primitive of times and totally unworthy of the head of a civilized nation.

29   He has forced our fellow citizens who were taken prisoner on the seas to bear arms against their country, to execute their own friends and family, or to be killed themselves.

30   He has stirred up rebellions among us here at home and has tried to turn the merciless Indian savages—whose way of warfare is to destroy without regard to age, sex, and condition—against the settlers on the frontiers.

31   At every stage of this oppression, we have asked for relief in the most humble terms. Our repeated requests have been answered only by more harm. A prince, who in every way acts like a tyrant, is unfit to be the ruler of a free people.

32   We have tried, in vain, to get the attention of our British brothers.

33   We have warned them from time to time of attempts by their legislature to extend an unwarrantable jurisdiction over us. We have reminded them of the circumstances of our emigration and settlement here. We have appealed to their native justice and magnanimity, and we have conjured them by the ties of our common kindred to disavow these usurpations, which, would inevitably interrupt our connections and correspondence. They too have been deaf to the voice of justice and of consanguinity. We must, therefore, acquiesce in the necessity, which denounces our Separation, and hold them, as we hold the rest of mankind, Enemies in War, in Peace Friends.

34   We, therefore, the Representatives of the United States of America, in General Congress, Assembled, appealing to the Supreme Judge of the world for the rectitude of our intentions, do, in the Name, and by Authority of the good People of these Colonies, solemnly publish and declare, That these United Colonies are, and of Right ought to be Free and Independent States; that they are Absolved from all Allegiance to the British Crown, and that all political connection between them and the State of Great Britain, is and ought to be totally dissolved; and that as Free and Independent States, they have full Power to levy War, conclude Peace, contract Alliances, establish Commerce, and to do all other Acts and Things which Independent States may of right do. And for the support of this Declaration, with a firm reliance on the protection of Divine Providence, we mutually pledge to each other our Lives, our Fortunes and our sacred Honor.

33   We have warned them from time to time of attempts by their government to extend an unfair rule over us. We reminded them why we came and settled here. We have appealed to their sense of justice and fair play. We asked them to remember our blood ties and not approve of these unlawful seizures of power which were bound to destroy our relationships with them. They have ignored us also. We must, therefore, hold them, as we hold the rest of mankind, to be enemies in war and friends in peacetime.

34   We, therefore, the representatives of the United States of America, brought together in a General Congress, appeal to the Supreme Judge of the world for the justice of our cause. In the name and by the authority of the good people of these colonies, we formally declare that these united colonies are—and have a right to be—free and independent states. We declare that they are freed of all loyalty to the British crown, and that all political connection between them and the state of Great Britain is—and should be—totally ended. As free and independent states they have full power to wage war, to make peace, to enter into alliances, to trade, and to do all the things that independent states have a right to do. Firmly relying on Divine Providence, we support this declaration and each pledge to the others our lives, our fortunes, and our sacred honor.

To His Excellency, General Washington

Phillis Wheatley

1   Celestial choir! enthron'd in realms of light,
Columbia's scenes of glorious toils I write.
While freedom's cause her anxious breast alarms,
She flashes dreadful in refulgent arms.
See mother earth her offspring's fate bemoan,
And nations gaze at scenes before unknown!
See the bright beams of heaven's revolving light
Involved in sorrows and the veil of night!

2   The goddess comes, she moves divinely fair,
Olive and laurel binds her golden hair;
Wherever shines this native of the skies,
Unnumber'd charms and recent graces rise.

3   Muse! bow propitious while my pen relates
How pour her armies through a thousand gates,
As when Eolus heaven's fair face deforms,
Enwrapp'd in tempest and a night of storms;
Astonis'd ocean feels the wild uproar,
The refluent surges beat the sounding shore;
Or thick as leaves in Autumn's golden reign,
Such, and so many, moves the warrior's train.

To His Excellency, General Washington

Phillis Wheatley

1   The poem is addressed to the angels in heaven ("celestial choir") who sit on thrones of light. In the first verse the speaker appeals to heaven, and to angels, bathed in light, to pay attention to America's glorious deeds. America's cause is freedom, and though she is anxious about fighting, she is prepared to do so if she must. The speaker says that even Mother Earth sympathizes with America as she stands at the center of world attention. In the midst of all this, the sun's "bright beams" shine on America's troubles.

2   In the short second verse, a goddess comes to bless and protect America. She comes with signs of peace and victory ("olive and laurel") in her hair and wherever she shines her light, blessings flow.

3   In the third verse the speaker calls on her poetic ability, to help her describe the movements of powerful armies. She compares the movement of the armies to winds (Eolus is the Greek god of the winds) moving across the ocean, causing great waves to beat upon the shore. Next, she describes the great number of warriors in Washington's army to be as "thick as leaves" in autumn. The army is seeking the "work of

In bright array they seek the work of war,
Where high unfurl'd the ensign waves in air.
Shall I to Washington their praise recite?
Enough thou know'st them in the fields of fight.
Thee, first in peace and honors,—we demand
The grace and glory of thy martial band.
Fam'd for thy valor, for thy virtues more,
Hear every tongue thy guardian aid implore!

4   One century scarce perform'd its destined round,
When Gallic powers Columbia's fury found;
And so may you, whoever dares disgrace
The land of freedom's heaven-defended race!
Fix'd are the eyes of nations on the scales,
For in their hopes Columbia's arm prevails.
Anon Britannia droops the pensive head,
While round increase the rising hills of dead.
Ah! cruel blindness to Columbia's state!
Lament thy thirst of boundless power too late.

5   Proceed, great chief, with virtue on thy side,
Thy ev'ry action let the goddess guide.
A crown, a mansion, and a throne that shine,
With gold unfading, WASHINGTON! be thine.

war" and waving its flag in the air. The speaker wonders if she should praise this army to Washington. She calls upon the goddess to bring "grace and glory" and to guard, aid, and protect the army.

4   Less than a century ago, the French were defeated in America. The same thing will happen to anyone who shames or mistreats the people in this land of freedom, for Heaven itself defends America. The eyes of the world are on this battle, and America carries their hopes and fears. Soon Britain's head will "droop" when she sees how many of her men have been killed. Finally (but too late), Britain will regret having used "boundless power" on America.

5   The final verse is an encouragement to Washington to "proceed." Right and virtue are on America's side. The speaker tells Washington to let the goddess guide his every action and then he will reap the rewards: a crown, a mansion, and a throne—all of gold.

from Letters from an American Farmer

Michel-Guillaume Jean de Crèvecoeur

1 *I*n this great American asylum, the poor of Europe have by some means met together, and in consequence of various causes; to what purpose should they ask one another, what countrymen they are? Alas, two-thirds of them had no country. Can a wretch who wanders about, who works and starves, whose life is a continual scene of sore affliction or pinching penury—can that man call England or any other kingdom his country? A country that had no bread for him, whose fields procured him no harvest, who met with nothing but the frowns of the rich, the severity of the laws, with jails and punishments, who owned not a single foot of the extensive surface of this planet? No! urged by a variety of

2 motives, here they came. Everything had tended to regenerate them: new laws, a new mode of living, a new social system. Here they are become men; in Europe they were as so many useless plants, wanting vegetative mold and refreshing showers; they withered and were mowed down by want, hunger, and war. But now, by the power of transplantation, like all other plants, they have taken root and flourished! Formerly they were not numbered in any civil list of their country, except in those of the poor; here they rank as citizens.

from Letters from an American Farmer

Michel-Guillaume Jean de Crèvecoeur

1   The poor people of Europe came to the shelter of America for many different reasons. When they meet, why should they ask one another about their previous citizenship? Two-thirds of them actually had no country. Can a miserable wanderer who works and starves, and whose life knows only sorrow and poverty—can that man call England or any other kingdom his country? His country had no bread for him, and the fields gave him no harvest. All he had were the frowns of the rich, harsh laws, jails, and punishments. Did he own even a single foot of the whole wide earth? No!

2   People were drawn to America for a variety of reasons. Everything here makes them feel reborn—new laws, a new way of living, a new social system. Here they become men. In Europe they were like useless plants. Without fertilizer and rain they withered and were mowed down by poverty, hunger, and war. But now that they are transplanted, they have taken root and blossomed! Before, they were not counted in any census of their country, except as the poor. Here they are called citizens.

3   What attachment can a poor European emigrant have for a country where he had nothing? The knowledge of the language, the love of a few kindred as poor as himself were the only cords that tied him. His country is now that which gives him land, bread, protection, and consequence. *Ubi panis ibi patria* [where my bread is earned, there is my country] is the motto of all emigrants. What then is the American, this new man? He is either a European or the descendant of a European; hence that strange mixture of blood which you will find in no other country. I could point out to you a man whose grandfather was an Englishman, whose wife was Dutch, whose son married a French woman, and whose present four sons have now four wives of different nations. *He* is an American who, leaving behind him all his ancient prejudices and manners, receives new ones from the new mode of life he has embraced, the new government he obeys, and the new rank he holds. He becomes an American by being received in the broad lap of our great alma mater.

4   Here individuals of all nations are melted into a new race of men, whose labors and posterity will one day cause great change in the world. Americans are the western pilgrims who are carrying along with them that great mass of arts, sciences, vigor, and industry which began long since in the east; they will finish the great circle. The Americans were once scattered all over Europe; here they are incorporated into one of the finest systems of population which has ever appeared, and which will hereafter become distinct by the power of the different climates they inhabit. The American ought, therefore, to love this country much better than that wherein either he or his forefathers were born. Here the rewards of his industry follow with equal steps the progress of his labor; his labor is

3   Why would a poor European emigrant feel connected to a country where he had nothing? The language and the love of a few poor relatives are his only ties. His new country gives him land, bread, protection, and importance. *Ubi panis ibi patria* [my country is where I earn my living] is the motto of all emigrants. What then is the American, this new man? He is either a European or the descendant of a European. There is a strange mixture of blood which you will find in no other country. I could point out to you a man whose grandfather was an Englishman, whose wife was Dutch, whose one son married a Frenchwoman, and whose other four sons have four wives from different nations. An American leaves behind all his old prejudices and customs and takes on new ones from the new way of life he has embraced, the new government he obeys, and the new rank he holds. He becomes an American by being gathered into the wide lap of the great, good mother.

4   Here, people from all nations are melted into a new race of men, whose work and descendants will one day bring great change to the world. Americans are the western pilgrims that carry along the main body of the arts and sciences and the great strength and hard work that began long ago in the East. They will finish the great circle. The Americans were once scattered across Europe. Here they are united into one of the finest populations that has ever appeared, a population that will be unique from now on because of their different backgrounds. The American should, therefore, love this country much better than the land where either he or his ancestors were born. Here the rewards of his work match his efforts. His work is based on natural self-interest. Could there be

founded on the basis of nature, self-interest. Can it want a stronger allurement? Wives and children, who before in vain demanded of him a morsel of bread, now, fat and frolicsome, gladly help their father to clear those fields whence exuberant crops are to arise to feed and to clothe them all, without any part being claimed, either by a despotic prince, a rich abbot, or a mighty lord. Here, religion demands but little of him; a small voluntary salary to the minister, and gratitude to God. Can he refuse these?

5   The American is a new man, who acts upon new principles; he must, therefore, entertain new ideas and form new opinions. From involuntary idleness, servile dependence, penury, and useless labor he has passed to toils of a very different nature, rewarded by ample subsistence. This is an American.

a stronger pull? Wives and children who could not demand even a small piece of bread from him in the past are now fat and happy. They gladly help their father clear the fields where an abundance of crops will grow to feed and clothe them all. No part of the profit can be claimed by a prince with unlimited powers, a rich religious leader, or a mighty lord. Here, religion takes only a little from him—a small voluntary contribution to the minister and gratitude to God. Can he refuse those?

5   The American is a new man who acts upon new principles. He must, therefore, think new ideas and form new opinions. From a life in which he was unable to work and in which he was dependent, poor, and useless, he now has good work that is rewarded by a good living. This is an American.

from
The Interesting Narrative of the Life of Olaudah Equiano

Gustavus Vassa

1   *T*he first object which saluted my eyes when I arrived on the coast, was the sea, and a slave ship, which was then riding at anchor, and waiting for its cargo. These filled me with astonishment, which was soon converted into terror, when I was carried on board. I was immediately handled, and tossed up to see if I were sound, by some of the crew; and I was now persuaded that I

2   had gotten into a world of bad spirits, and that they were going to kill me. Their complexions, too, differing so much from ours, their long hair, and the language they spoke (which was very different from any I had ever heard), united to confirm me in this belief. Indeed, such were the horrors of my views and

from
The Interesting Narrative of the Life of Olaudah Equiano

Gustavus Vassa

From 1619 until the slave trade was outlawed in 1808, millions of Africans were brought to America against their will. In an autobiography written in 1791, Gustavus Vassa (formerly named Olaudah Equiano), recounts his capture and forced immigration to the United States. This narrative begins shortly before he is carried aboard a slave ship.

1   The first object I saw when I arrived on the coast was the sea and a slave ship that was anchored and waiting for its cargo. I was astonished by these sights, but that feeling was soon replaced by terror when I was carried on board. I was immediately examined and tossed around by some of the crew to see how healthy I was.

2   I now realized that I had gotten into a world of bad spirits, and that they were going to kill me. The crew's skin color, long hair, and language were so different from our own that I was sure my worst fears were true. Indeed, in that moment, I was so horrified and afraid that if I had owned 10,000 worlds I would

fears at the moment, that, if ten thousand worlds
had been my own, I would have freely parted with
them all to have exchanged my condition with that of
3   the meanest slave in my own country. When I looked
round the ship too, and saw a large furnace of copper
boiling, and a multitude of black people of every
description chained together, every one of their countenances expressing dejection and sorrow, I no longer
doubted of my fate; and, quite overpowered with horror and anguish, I fell motionless on the deck and
fainted. When I recovered a little, I found some black
people about me, who I believed were some of those
who had brought me on board, and had been receiving their pay; they talked to me in order to cheer me,
but all in vain. I asked them if we were not to be
eaten by those white men with horrible looks, red
faces, and long hair. They told me I was not, and one
4   of the crew brought me a small portion of spirituous
liquor in a wine glass; but, being afraid of him, I
would not take it out of his hand. One of the blacks,
therefore, took it from him and gave it to me, and I
took a little down my palate, which, instead of reviving me, as they thought it would, threw me into the
greatest consternation at the strange feeling it produced, having never tasted any such liquor before.
Soon after this, the blacks who brought me on board
went off, and left me abandoned to despair.

5   I now saw myself deprived of all chance of
returning to my native country, or even the least
glimpse of hope of gaining the shore, which I now
considered as friendly; and I even wished for my former slavery in preference to my present situation,
which was filled with horrors of every kind, still
heightened by my ignorance of what I was to
undergo. I was not long suffered to indulge my grief;
I was soon put down under the decks, and there I

have gladly given them away and traded places with the poorest slave in my own country.

3   As I looked around the ship, I saw a large furnace of copper boiling and a great many black people of every description chained together. Every one of their faces showed dejection and sorrow. I no longer doubted my fate. Overpowered with horror and anguish, I fainted on the deck. When I recovered, some of the black people who had brought me on board were standing around me. They had just received their pay. They tried to talk to me and cheer me up, but it didn't help. I asked them if we might be eaten by those white men with the horrible looks, red faces, and long hair. They told me that wasn't true.

4   One of the crew brought me a small drink of liquor in a wine glass, but I was afraid of him. I would not take it out of his hand, so one of the blacks took it from the crew member and gave it to me. I drank a little of it. Instead of reviving me, as they thought it would, it upset me greatly because of the strange feeling it produced. I had never tasted liquor like this before. Soon, the blacks who brought me on board went away and left me alone with my despair.

5   I now saw that I had no chance of returning to my native country and no hope of getting to shore. I would have preferred my former slavery to this situation, for it was filled with horrors of every kind that were exaggerated by my not knowing what would come next. I could not dwell on my grief for very long for I was soon put below deck, and my nostrils received a greeting such as I had never experienced in my life. The disgusting stench combined with the

received such a salutation in my nostrils as I had never experienced in my life: so that, with the loath-someness of the stench, and crying together, I became so sick and low that I was not able to eat, nor had I the least desire to taste anything. I now wished for the last friend, death, to relieve me; but soon, to my grief, two of the white men offered me

6 eatables; and, on my refusing to eat, one of them held me fast by the hands, and laid me across, I think, the windlass, and tied my feet, while the other flogged me severely. I had never experienced anything of this kind before, and, although not being used to the water, I naturally feared that element the first time I saw it, yet, nevertheless, could I have got over the nettings, I would have jumped over the side, but I could not; and besides, the crew used to watch us very closely who were not chained down to the decks, lest we should leap into the water; and I have seen some of these poor African prisoners most severely cut, for attempting to do so, and hourly whipped for not eating. This indeed was often the

7 case with myself. In a little time after, amongst the poor chained men, I found some of my own nation, which in a small degree gave ease to my mind. I inquired of these what was to be done with us? They gave me to understand, we were to be carried to these white people's country to work for them. I then was a little revived, and thought, if it were no worse than working, my situation was not so desperate; but still I feared I should be put to death, the white people looked and acted, as I thought, in so savage a manner; for I had never seen among any people such instances of brutal cruelty; and this not only shown towards us blacks, but also to some of the whites themselves. One white man in particular I saw, when we were permitted to be on deck, flogged so unmercifully with a large rope near the foremast,

crying made me so sick and discouraged that I was not able to eat, nor did I have the least bit of appetite. Now I wished that death, the last friend, would relieve me, but soon, to my grief, two of the white men offered me food to eat.

6   When I refused to eat, one of them held me tight by the hands and laid me across a windlass[1] and tied my feet, while the other gave me a beating with a whip. I had never experienced anything like this before. Although I was not used to water and feared it the first time I saw it, I would have jumped over the side if I could have gotten over the nets, but I could not. Besides, the crew watched us very closely when we were not chained down to the decks, lest we should leap into the water. I have seen some of these poor African prisoners badly cut for attempting to do so, and whipped hourly for not eating. Indeed, this was often the case with me.

7   A little while later, among the poor chained men, I found some of my own countrymen, which gave me a little comfort. I asked them what would happen with us. They told me that we were to be carried to these white people's country to work for them. I felt a little better and thought if it were no worse than working, then my situation was not so desperate. But I was still afraid that I would be killed, for the white people looked and acted like savages. I had never seen such instances of brutal cruelty among any people, not only toward us blacks, but also toward some of the whites themselves. In particular, one white man that I saw, when we were permitted to be on deck, was beaten so severely with a large rope near the

---

1 **windlass:** apparatus that is used for hauling or hoisting rope or chain on a ship

that he died in consequence of it; and they tossed him over the side as they would have done a brute.

8   This made me fear these people the more; and I expected nothing less than to be treated in the same manner. I could not help expressing my fears and apprehensions to some of my countrymen; I asked them if these people had no country, but lived in this hollow place (the ship)? They told me they did not, but came from a distant one. "Then," said I, "how comes it in all our country we never heard of them?" They told me because they lived so very far off. I then asked where were their women? had they any like themselves? I was told they had. "And why," said I, "do we not see them?" They answered, because they were left behind. I asked how the vessel could

9   go? They told me they could not tell; but that there was cloth put upon the masts by the help of the ropes I saw, and then the vessel went on; and the white men had some spell or magic they put in the water when they liked, in order to stop the vessel. I was exceedingly amazed at this account, and really thought they were spirits. I therefore wished much to be from amongst them, for I expected they would sacrifice me; but my wishes were vain—for we were so quartered that it was impossible for any of us to make our escape.

10   While we stayed on the coast I was mostly on deck; and one day, to my great astonishment, I saw one of these vessels coming in with the sails up. As soon as the whites saw it, they gave a great shout, at which we were amazed; and the more so, as the vessel appeared larger by approaching nearer. At last, she

foremast[2] that he died from the beating, and they tossed him overboard as if he were an animal.

8   This made me fear these people even more, and I expected nothing less than to be treated in the same way. I could not help expressing my great fears to some of my countrymen. I asked them if the white men had no country but lived in the ship. They told me the white men came from a distant country. "Then," I said, "why have we never heard of them in our country?" They told me that it was because the white men lived so far away. I then asked where their women were and if they had any women. I was told they had. "And why," I said, "do we not see them?" They answered that the women were left behind.

9   I asked how the ship moved. They told me they did not know but that there was cloth put upon the masts by the help of the ropes I saw. In this way the ship went on, and the white men had some spell or magic they put in the water when they wanted to, in order to stop the ship. I was greatly amazed at this report and really thought the white men were spirits. I wished I were away from them, for I expected they would sacrifice me, but nothing came of my wishes. We were confined in such a way that it was impossible for any of us to make our escape.

10   I stayed mostly on deck while we were on the coast and one day, to my great surprise, I saw one of these ships coming in with her sails up. As soon as the whites saw it, they gave a great shout. We were more and more amazed as the ship grew larger as it approached us. At last I saw her drop anchor. I and my countrymen were completely astonished to see

2 **foremast:** tall vertical pole that supports the sails and is located nearest the front of the ship

came to an anchor in my sight, and when the anchor
was let go, I and my countrymen who saw it, were lost
in astonishment to observe the vessel stop—and were
now convinced it was done by magic. Soon after this
the other ship got her boats out, and they came on
board of us, and the people of both ships seemed very
glad to see each other. Several of the strangers also
shook hands with us black people, and made motions
with their hands, signifying I suppose, we were to go
to their country, but we did not understand them.

11   At last, when the ship we were in, had got in all
her cargo, they made ready with many fearful
noises, and we were all put under deck, so that we
could not see how they managed the vessel. But this
disappointment was the least of my sorrow. The
stench of the hold while we were on the coast was so
intolerably loathsome, that it was dangerous to
remain there for any time, and some of us had been
permitted to stay on the deck for the fresh air; but
now that the whole ship's cargo were confined
together, it became absolutely pestilential. The closeness of the place, and the heat of the climate, added
to the number in the ship, which was so crowded
that each had scarcely room to turn himself, almost
suffocated us. This produced copious perspirations,
12   so that the air soon became unfit for respiration,
from a variety of loathsome smells, and brought on a
sickness among the slaves, of which many died—
thus falling victims to the improvident avarice, as I
may call it, of their purchasers. This wretched situation as again aggravated by the galling of the
chains, now became insupportable, and the filth of
the necessary tubs, into which the children often fell,
and were almost suffocated. The shrieks of the
women, and the groans of the dying, rendered the
whole a scene of horror almost inconceivable.

the ship come to a stop—and were convinced it was done by magic. Soon, the other ship got her boats out, and they came on board our ship. The crew of both ships seemed very glad to see each other. Several of the strangers also shook hands with us black people and made hand gestures that said, I suppose, that we were to go to their country, but we did not understand them.

11   At last when our ship had loaded in all her cargo, the crew made fearful noises, and we were all put below deck so we could not see how they managed the ship. But this disappointment was my smallest sorrow. The stench of this below-deck prison while we were on the coast was so incredibly disgusting that is was dangerous to stay there for any time, and some of us had been permitted to stay on the deck for the fresh air. But now that all of the ship's cargo was packed into one place, the atmosphere became deadly. The closeness of this space, the heat of the climate, and the number of people in the ship (which was so crowded that each had scarcely room to turn) almost suffocated us.

12   People sweat so much that the air soon became unfit for breathing from a variety of awful smells. Many slaves became sick and died—victims of the reckless greed of those who had bought them. This horrible situation, made even worse by the constant irritation of the chains, now became unbearable. Children often fell into the filthy tubs used for bodily waste and were almost suffocated. The shrieks of the women and the groans of the dying made the place a scene of horror almost impossible to imagine.

13   Happily perhaps, for myself, I was soon reduced so low here that it was thought necessary to keep me almost always on deck; and from my extreme youth I was not put in fetters. In this situation I expected every hour to share the fate of my companions, some of whom were almost daily brought upon deck at the point of death, which I began to hope would soon put an end to my miseries. Often did I think many of the inhabitants of the deep much more happy than myself. I envied them the freedom they enjoyed, and as often wished I could change my condition for theirs. Every circumstance I met with, served only to render my state more painful, and heightened my apprehensions, and my opinion of the cruelty of the whites.

14   During our passage, I first saw flying fishes, which surprised me very much; they used frequently to fly across the ship, and many of them fell on the deck. I also now first saw the use of the quadrant; I had often with astonishement seen the mariners make observations with it, and I could not think what it meant. They at last took notice of my surpirse; and one of them, willing to increase it, as well as to gratify my curiosity, made me one day look through it. The clouds appeared to me to be land, which disappeared as they passed along. This heightened my wonder; and I was now more persuaded than ever, that I was in another world, and that every thing about me was magic. At last, we came in

15   sight of the island of Barbadoes, at which the whites on board gave a great shout, and made many signs of joy to us. We did not know what to think of this; but as the vessel drew nearer, we plainly saw the harbor, and other ships of different kinds and sizes, and we soon anchored amongst them, off Bridgetown. Many

13   Luckily for me, perhaps, I was soon in such bad shape that they thought it was necessary to keep me almost always on deck, and because of my young age I was not put in chains. Every hour I expected to share the fate of my fellow prisoners. Some of them were almost daily brought upon deck at the point of death, which I began to hope would soon put an end to my miseries. I often thought that the inhabitants of the deep sea were much happier than I was. I envied them their freedom and often wished I could change places with them. Every situation I met only added to my pain and raised my fears of the cruelty of the whites.

14   During our passage I first saw flying fish, which surprised me very much. They frequently flew across the ship, and many of them fell on the deck. I also saw the quadrant[3] used for the first time. I had often been amazed to see the sailors make observations with the quadrant, and I did not know what it meant. Finally they noticed my surprise and one of them who wanted to surprise me even more, as well as to satisfy my curiosity, made me look through it one day. The clouds looked like land to me and disappeared as they passed along. This raised my sense of wonder, and I was more convinced than ever that I was in another world, and that everything around me was magic.

15   At last we came in sight of the island of Barbados, which caused the whites on board to shout and make signs of joy to us. We did not know what to think of this, but as the ship drew nearer, we saw the harbor clearly and other ships of different kinds and sizes. We soon anchored among them, off Bridgetown.

3 **quadrant:** instrument used for measuring the height of objects above sea level

merchants and planters now came on board, though it was in the evening. They put us in separate parcels, and examined us attentively. They also made us jump, and pointed to the land, signifying we were to go there. We thought by this, we should be eaten by these ugly men, as they appeared to us; and, when 16 soon after we were all put down under the deck again, there was much dread and trembling among us, and nothing but bitter cries to be heard all the night from these apprehensions, insomuch, that at last the white people got some old slaves from the land to pacify us. They told us we were not to be eaten, but to work, and were soon to go on land, where we would see many of our country people. This report eased us much. And sure enough, soon after we were landed, there came to us Africans of all languages.

17   We were conducted immediately to the merchant's yard, were we were all pent up together, like so many sheep in a fold, without regard to sex or age. As every object was new to me, everything I saw filled me with surprise. What struck me first, was, that the houses were built with bricks and stories, and in every other respect different from those I had seen in Africa; but I was still more astonished on seeing people on horseback. I did not know what this could mean; and, indeed, I thought these people were full of nothing but magical arts. While I was in this astonishment, one of my fellow prisoners spoke to a countryman of his, about the horses, who said they were the same kind they had in their country. I understood them, though they were from a distant part of Africa; and I thought it odd I had not seen any horses there; but afterwards, which I came to converse with different Africans, I found they had many horses amongst them, and much larger than those I then saw.

Many merchants and planters came on board, though it was evening. They put us in separate groups and examined us with great care. They also made us jump and pointed to the land, indicating that we were to go there. We thought we would be eaten by these ugly-appearing men.

16   Soon after we were all put below deck again, and there was much fear and trembling among us. Nothing but bitter cries could be heard all night until at last the white people brought some old slaves from the land to calm us down. They told us we were not to be eaten, but to work. Soon we would go on land where we would see many people from our own country. Their report quieted us. And sure enough, soon after we landed, Africans of all languages came to us.

17   We were taken immediately to the merchant's yard, where we were all kept in a pen, like so many sheep, without any attention to sex or age. Because everything was new to me, everything I saw surprised me. What struck me first was that the houses were built with bricks and in stories and that in every way they were different from those I had seen in Africa. I was even more amazed at seeing people on horseback. I did not know what this meant, and I was sure these people had all the magical arts. While I was thinking of these wonders, one of my fellow prisoners spoke to a countryman about horses. He said the horses were the same kind as they had in their country. I understood this conversation, though these people were from a distant part of Africa. I thought it was odd that I had not seen any horses in Africa but after talking with different Africans, I found that they had many horses among them, even larger ones than those I saw.

18   We were not many days in the merchant's custody, before we were sold after their usual manner, which is this: On a signal given (as the beat of a drum), the buyers rush at once into the yard where the slaves are confined, and make choice of that parcel they like best. The noise and clamor with which this is attended, and the eagerness visible in the countenances of the buyers, serve not a little to increase the apprehension of terrified Africans, who may well be supposed to consider them as the ministers of that destruction to which they think themselves devoted. In this manner, without scruple, are relations and friends separated, most of them never to see each other again. I remember, in the vessel in which I was brought over, in the men's apartment, there were several brothers, who, in the sale, were sold in different lots; and it was very moving on this occasion, to see and hear their cries at

19 parting. O, ye nominal Christians! might not an African ask you—Learned you this from your God, who says unto you, Do unto all men as you would men should do unto you? Is it not enough that we are torn from our country and friends, to toil for your luxury and lust of gain? Must every tender feeling be likewise sacrificed to your avarice? Are the dearest friends and relations, now rendered more dear by their separation from their kindred, still to be parted from each other, and thus prevented from cheering the gloom of slavery, with the small comfort of being together, and mingling their sufferings and sorrows? Why are parents to lose their children, brothers their sisters, or husbands their wives? Surely, this is a new refinement in cruelty, which, while it has not advantage to atone for it, thus aggravates distress, and adds fresh horrors even to the wretchedness of slavery.

18   After a few days in the merchant's custody, we were sold in the usual manner, which is this: After a signal (such as the beat of a drum), the buyers rush into the yard where the slaves are held, and choose the group of slaves they like best. The noise, commotion, and the eagerness on the faces of the buyers, increase the fears of the terrified Africans, who see the merchants as ministers of destruction. Without the slightest tweak of conscience, relatives and friends are separated, most of them never to see each other again. I remember that in the ship I was brought over in there were several brothers in the men's section who were sold in different lots in the sale. It was very moving to see and hear their cries as they parted.

19   O, all of you who say you are Christians! Might not an African ask you—did you learn this from your God, who tells you to do unto all men as you would have men do unto you? Isn't it enough that we are torn from our country and our friends to work for your luxury and greed? Does every tender feeling need to be sacrificed to this greed? Must our dearest friends and relatives, now more precious because of our separation from our familes back home, be separated from us? Must we be prevented from lifting the gloom of slavery with the small comfort of being together and sharing our sufferings and sorrows? Why must parents lose their children, brothers their sisters, or husbands their wives? Surely, this is a new type of cruelty, which cannot be justified as giving the owners any advantage. It only worsens our distress and adds fresh horrors to the wretchedness of slavery.

Unit Three
A Growing Nation
(1800–1870)

*T*hrough wars, treaties, and agreements such as the Louisiana Purchase in 1803, more and more land was added to the country which now stretched from coast to coast and from Canada to the Rio Grande in Texas.

Extending Civil Rights

As the nineteenth century began, the common man took center stage on the American political scene. The original U.S. Constitution granted basic civil rights to a small class of property-owning, tax-paying white men. As the country expanded, the idea of extending civil rights to other groups of citizens grew. Andrew Jackson, elected president in 1828, became known as the champion of the common man. Under his administration the right to vote was granted to all free men for the first time in our nation's history.

When that happened, some people began asking how a democracy that valued freedom for some could tolerate slavery for others. Abolitionists, people opposed to slavery, began organizing anti-slavery societies and publishing anti-slavery newspapers. Frederick Douglass, a fugitive slave, published his

Narrative in the Life of Frederick Douglass in 1845.
Anti-slavery leaders used it to show the horrors of slavery, and Douglass became the most famous abolitionist in the United States.

Women who were active in the abolitionist movement also began to question their status in society. In 1848 they organized the first women's rights convention in Seneca Falls, New York. At the meeting they read a Declaration of Independence, which stated that all men *and women* are created equal. It was a revolutionary idea for the time.

Other ideas and inventions shaped the growing nation. Many people began to support the idea of free public education. Inventions such as the steamboat by Robert Fuller in 1802 and the telegraph by Samuel Morse in 1836 made transportation and communication across the country easier and faster. The invention of the cotton gin at the end of the eighteenth century led to an increase in slave labor in the South. In the North, textile factories sprang up that depended on a huge supply of cotton from the South and on cheap labor in the North.

Transcendentalists and Fireside Poets

One of the most popular ideas among American writers of the time was transcendentalism. This philosophy, like the ideas of the Age of Reason, had its roots in Europe. The transcendentalists believed in a God who was as close as one's own breath—a God within the human spirit and all of nature. Intuition, self-reliance, and originality were important aspects of this new thought. Its most respected spokesperson was a minister turned philosopher named Ralph Waldo Emerson.

Emerson's most famous student was his neighbor, Henry David Thoreau. Unlike Emerson, who was outgoing and charming, Thoreau was introverted and odd. Yet Thoreau lived what Emerson preached. For two years, Thoreau lived apart from society in a simple cabin in the woods. Excerpts from his most famous works, "Civil Disobedience" and *Walden* are included in this unit.

Better known in their time than today were the poets of the nineteenth century. Gathering around the fireplace and reading poetry aloud was a common family entertainment. For this reason, a small group of especially popular poets came to be known as the "Fireside Poets." Henry Wadsworth Longfellow was the best known and most beloved of the Fireside Poets. The others were Oliver Wendell Holmes, James Russell Lowell, John Greenleaf Whittier, and William Cullen Bryant.

The Civil War

The middle of the century saw the inevitable coming of the Civil War (1861–1865). Though the nation had tried to sidestep the issue of slavery, in the end it could not. After years of debating the issue in the halls of Congress, the nation was at war.

For four years the war dragged on. The Battle of Gettysburg, midpoint in the war, was one of the bloodiest of all the Civil War battles. In December of 1863 President Abraham Lincoln gave the Gettysburg Address, a speech that is part of this unit. The speech was so short that newspapers of the day shrugged it off as insignificant. Today we recognize that in a few carefully-chosen, eloquent words Lincoln captured the spirit of that war-weary time.

At the end of the war Robert E. Lee, leader of the Confederate States of America, also captured a pivotal time in history with a brief speech. Lee's "Farewell to the Army," included in this unit, broke the news to his bedraggled troops that the awful war was finally over, and they could go home again.

The world they went home to was forever changed. Out of the ashes of the war rose new industry, new political alliances, new hopes and dreams, and new problems.

Unit Three Author Biographies

William Cullen Bryant   1794–1878

William Cullen Bryant's most famous poem on death, "Thanatopsis," won him early fame but not fortune. He could not make a living as a poet and practiced law to support himself. In 1821 his first book of poetry appeared. Four years later he joined the New York literary scene as editor of the *New York Review* and *Atheneum Magazine*. The magazines folded, but Bryant was soon assistant editor and then part owner and editor in chief of the *New York Evening Post*. From this position he built the newspaper into one of the most respected in the nation. Bryant spoke out strongly against the institution of slavery and in favor of Abraham Lincoln's presidency.

Ralph Waldo Emerson   1803–1882

Ralph Waldo Emerson was one of this country's greatest thinkers. Descended from seven generations of ministers, he tried the ministry but quit after his wife died and his faith faltered. After traveling in Europe, Emerson came back and began to write poems and essays that soon got him noticed. He also lectured widely and formed the Transcendental Club with some friends. They believed in the dignity of the individual and the importance of being true to oneself rather than following the rules of any organized religion. Emerson's first book, *Nature*, laid out the ideas of transcendentalism. In 1841 he published his *Essays* and with it gained a worldwide reputation.

Henry David Thoreau   1817–1862

Henry David Thoreau was an original thinker who was considered an eccentric and a failure during his short lifetime. The truth is that he was ahead of his time.

Like his friend Emerson, Thoreau believed in self-reliance and following his conscience rather than blind authority. This often put him at odds with both his neighbors and society. He once spent a night in jail because he refused to pay a poll tax that would support the Mexican War, which he opposed. For two years he lived by himself in a simple cabin in the woods. His observations and experiences there form the basis for one of the two books, *Walden*, which were published during his life. Though his genius was not recognized while he was alive, his ideas on civil disobedience, materialism, and conservation have both irritated and challenged today's readers.

Henry Wadsworth Longfellow   1807–1882

Henry Wadsworth Longfellow was perhaps the most loved poet of the nineteeth century. At 28 Longfellow published his first volume of poetry, and he was soon popular with the public and critics alike. His subject matter ranged from mythology to the classics and from European and American folklore to historic and patriotic themes.

Oliver Wendell Holmes   1809–1894

Oliver Wendell Holmes was only 21 years old when he wrote "Old Ironsides," the poem contained in this unit. Holmes was, by profession, a highly-respected physician, but he also wrote popular poetry, essays, and novels. With his friend, James Russell Lowell, Holmes established the *Atlantic Monthly* magazine. Holmes was a jolly and popular after-dinner speaker and associated with most of the other famous writers and poets of his day. Though "Old Ironsides" is a serious poem, most of Holmes' poems are not. They do not have a tight rhyme scheme and are usually lighthearted and witty.

James Russell Lowell
1819–1891

James Russell Lowell was a popular nineteenth-century poet who was involved in two of the most important social causes of his day: the anti-slavery movement and the early women's rights movement. In 1857 he became editor of the *Atlantic Monthly*, one of the most influential magazines in the country. His breakthrough book was a satire on America's attitudes toward Mexico and the Southern states' attempts to expand slavery into the Southwest. Its publication in 1848 helped change the minds of many Northerners on these issues.

John Greenleaf Whittier
1807–1892

Unlike his fellow poets Longfellow and Lowell, John Greenleaf Whittier did not have the benefits of a fine education or grow up among poets and writers. He was, however, an avid reader. At 19 his first poem was published, and at 26 his first book, *Legends of New England*, was published. A devout Quaker, Whittier was also strongly against the institution of slavery. He supported himself by working for anti-slavery newspapers and was stoned, mobbed, and shot at for his work in this cause.

Frederick Douglass
1817–1895

Frederick Douglass was an eloquent and effective speaker against slavery. An escaped slave himself, he published his *Narrative on the Life of Frederick Douglass* in 1845. It received so much attention that Douglass feared his former owner might try to recapture him, and left the country. After two years abroad, Douglass's friends bought his freedom for $700, and he returned home to resume his work against the institution of slavery. Douglass published the first

African-American newspaper in this country around 1847. His deeds matched his words. He helped slaves escape to Canada via the Underground Railroad and urged black soldiers to enlist in the Civil War. After the war he continued to speak out against injustice and to champion human rights.

Abraham Lincoln   1809–1865

Abraham Lincoln was president of the United States through its most troubling time in the country's history, the Civil War. With almost no formal education, Lincoln rose from poverty to president. His ability to tell a good story and enjoy a good laugh are legendary. His simple speaking and writing style was in sharp contrast to the flowery orators and writers of his day. A wise and shrewd leader, he steered a middle course through the years of his presidency. His second Inaugural Address and the Gettysburg Address have become standards among American political writings.

Robert E. Lee   1807–1870

Robert E. Lee was the commander in chief of the Confederate States of America. He is remembered as a military genius, whose strategies and tactics are still being studied today. Lee surrendered to General Grant of the Union forces in April 1865 at Appomattox Court House in Virginia. After the war he turned his attention to education and became president of Washington College, now Washington and Lee University. Though he was a well-educated and brilliant man, he did not give speeches, nor did he write his memoirs of the Civil War. What remains are some letters and, of course, the "Farewell to the Army" speech that is found in this unit. Lee applied for, but was never given, amnesty for his role in the war. In 1975 his citizenship was granted by an act of Congress.

Thanatopsis

William Cullen Bryant

1   To him who in the love of Nature holds
     Communion with her visible forms, she speaks
     A various language; for his gayer hours
     She has a voice of gladness, and a smile
     And eloquence of beauty, and she glides
2   Into his darker musings, with a mild
     And healing sympathy, that steals away
     Their sharpness, ere he is aware. When thoughts
     Of the last bitter hour come like a blight
     Over the spirit, and sad images
3   Of the stern agony, and shroud, and pall,
     And breathless darkness, and the narrow house,
     Make thee to shudder, and grow sick at heart;—
     Go forth, under the open sky, and list
     To Nature's teachings, while from all around—
4   Earth and her waters, and the depths of air—
     Comes a still voice—Yet a few days, and thee
     The all-beholding sun shall see no more
     In all his course; not yet in the cold ground,
     Where thy pale form was laid, with many tears,

5   Nor in the embrace of ocean, shall exist
     Thy image. Earth, that nourished thee, shall claim
     Thy growth, to be resolved to earth again,
     And, lost each human trace, surrendering up
     Thine individual being, shalt thou go

Thanatopsis

William Cullen Bryant

1   To the nature lover who feels
Closely connected with the earth, Nature speaks in
More than one language. For the happier times
Nature has a cheerful voice, a smile,
And eloquent beauty. Nature slips

2   Into a person's darker thoughts with a gentle
And healing understanding that takes away
The pain before a person realizes it. When thoughts
Of life's last bitter hour eat away at
Your spirit, and sad images

3   Of death's agony and funeral cloths,
And darkness without breath in a narrow grave
Make you shudder and feel depressed—
Go out under the open sky and listen
To Nature's teachings. From all around,

4   From the Earth and her seas and from the deepest
      part of the air—
Comes a quiet voice: In only a few days
The sun, which sees everyone, will see you no more
Along his path. Nor in the cold ground
Where your pale body was laid, with many tears,

5   Nor in the loving arms of the ocean will
You be known. The Earth that nourished you will
      claim
Your growth, to be changed into earth again,
And losing all trace of who you were, you will give up
Your individual being and will go

6   To mix for ever with the elements,
    To be a brother to the insensible rock
    And to the sluggish clod, which the rude swain
    Turns with his share, and treads upon. The oak
    Shall send his roots abroad, and pierce thy mold.

7   Yet not to thine eternal resting-place
    Shalt thou retire alone, nor couldst thou wish
    Couch more magnificent. Thou shalt lie down
    With patriarchs of the infant world—with kings,
    The powerful of the earth—the wise, the good,
8   Fair forms, and hoary seers of ages past,
    All in one mighty sepulchre. The hills
    Rock-ribbed and ancient as the sun—the vales
    Stretching in pensive quietness between;
    the venerable woods—rivers that move

9   In majesty, and the complaining brooks
    That make the meadows green; and, poured round
        all,
    Old Ocean's gray and melancholy waste,—
    Are but the solemn decorations all
    Of the great tomb of man. The golden sun,
10 The planets, all the infinite host of heaven,
    Are shining on the sad abodes of death,
    Through the still lapse of ages. All that tread
    The globe are but a handful to the tribes
    That slumber in its bosom.—Take the wings

11 Of morning, pierce the Barcan wilderness,
    Or lose thyself in the continuous woods
    Where rolls the Oregon, and hears no sound,
    Save his own dashings—yet the dead are there:
    And millions in those solitudes, since first

6   To mix forever with the elements,
    To be a brother to the non-feeling rock
    And to the clump of earth which the simple farm-
        worker
    Turns over with his plow and steps on. The oak
    Will send out its roots and cut through the mold that
        you have become.
7   Still, to your eternal resting place
    You will not go alone, nor could you wish
    For a more magnificent bed. You will lie down
    With the patriarchs of the ancient world—with kings,
    The powerful of the earth—the wise, the good,
8   The lovely ones, and the white-haired prophets of
        long ago,
    All in one great tomb. The hills
    Rocky-ridged and as old as the sun—the valleys
    Stretching in quiet sadness in between,
    Ancient woods—majestic rivers
9   And the noisy brooks
    That make the meadows green; and surrounding
        everything
    The old ocean's gray and gloomy expanse—
    These are all the sacred decorations
    Of the great tomb of man. The golden sun,
10 The planets, all the multitudes of angels
    Are shining on the sad resting places of death,
    Through the quiet passing away of time. Everyone
        who walks
    The earth is but a handful compared to the tribes of
        people
    Who sleep in earth's bosom. Take the wings
11 Of morning, break through the desert in North
        Africa,
    Or lose yourself in the deep woods
    Where the Oregon River does not hear a sound
    Except for its own ripplings—yet the dead are there.
    And millions in those isolated places, since time
        began, have laid down

12   The flight of years began, have laid them down
      In their sleep—the dead reign there alone,
      So shalt thou rest, and what if thou withdraw
      In silence from the living, and no friend
      Take note of thy departure? All that breathe

13   Will share thy destiny. The gay will laugh
      When thou art gone, the solemn brood of care
      Plod on, and each one as before will chase
      His favorite phantom, yet all these shall leave
      Their mirth and their employments, and shall come,

14   And make their bed with thee. As the long train
      Of ages glide away, the sons of men,
      The youth in life's green spring, and he who goes
      In the full strength of years, matron and maid,
      The speechless babe, and the gray-headed man—

15   Shall one by one be gathered to thy side,
      By those, who in their turn shall follow them.

16   So live that when thy summons comes to join
      The innumerable caravan, which moves
      To that mysterious realm, where each shall take
      His chamber in the silent halls of death,
      Thou go not, like the quarry-slave at night,
17   Scourged to his dungeon, but, sustained and soothed
      By an unfaltering trust,
          approach thy grave,
      Like one who wraps the
          drapery of his couch
      About him, and lies down
          to pleasant dreams.

12 In their last sleep—the dead rule by themselves
    there.
    So you will rest, and what if you pull back
    In silence from the living, and no friend
    Even notices that you have died? Everything that
    breathes
13 Will share your fate. The light-hearted will laugh
    When you are gone; the serious will keep
    Trudging along, and each will chase
    His favorite vain dream as he always has; yet all
    these will leave
    Their happiness and their business and will come
14 And make their bed with you. As the long line
    Of the ages moves along, the sons of men,
    Young people in the green spring of life, and the one
    who dies
    At the peak of life, married woman or young maid,
    The baby who has not learned to talk and the gray-
    headed man—
15 Will one by one be gathered to your side
    By those, who in their turn will follow.

16 So live! Then when your call comes to join
    The long caravan that moves
    To that mysterious place, where each will take
    A room in the silent halls of death,
    You do not go like the hunted slave at night
17 Driven back to a dungeon, but supported and
    comforted
    By a faith that does not waver, approach your grave
    Like someone who wraps a blanket from his bed
    Around himself and lies down to pleasant dreams.

Concord Hymn

Ralph Waldo Emerson

1   By the rude bridge
       that arched the
       flood,
    Their flag to
       April's breeze
       unfurled,
    Here once the
       embattled
       farmers stood,
    And fired the shot heard round the world.

2   The foe long since in silence slept;
    Alike the conqueror silent sleeps;
    And Time the ruined bridge has swept
    Down the dark stream which seaward creeps.

3   On this green bank, by this soft stream,
    We set to-day a votive stone;
    That memory may their deed redeem,
    When, like our sires, our sons are gone.

4   Spirit, that made those heroes dare
    To die, or leave their children free,
    Bid Time and Nature gently spare
    The shaft we raise to them and thee.

Concord Hymn

Ralph Waldo Emerson

1   The first line refers to a bridge (North Bridge) where the Battle of Concord was fought on April 19, 1775. Concord was the second battle (after Lexington) in the Revolutionary War, and the early victory at Concord greatly boosted morale among the Americans. This "rude bridge" is the spot where a group of American farmers stood their ground that April day, drove back the British, and "fired the shot heard round the world," the shot that started the Revolutionary War and inspired freedom-fighters around the world.

2   The second verse states that both the losers (the British) and the winners (the Americans) are long dead. Time has ruined the bridge and sent it drifting downstream to the sea. Likewise, the memory of this event has faded from American consciousness.

3   The third verse reminds the assembly of their purpose in gathering: to commemorate what happened on this site at the beginning of the Revolutionary War. A memorial stone is being set in place so that generations to come will remember this place, long after the sons of the people placing the stone are dead.

4   The final verse calls on the eternal spirit that inspired the men to bravely risk their lives for their chidren's freedom. The poem asks that both the spirit and nature preserve this memorial to the heroes at Concord and to the spirit who led them.

Self-Reliance

Ralph Waldo Emerson

1   *I* read the other day some verses written by an eminent painter which were original and not conventional. Always the soul hears an admonition in such lines, let the subject be what it may. The sentiment they instill is of more value than any thought they may contain. To believe your own thought, to believe that what is true for you in your private heart, is true for all men—that is genius. Speak your latent conviction and it shall be the universal sense; for always the inmost becomes the outmost, and our first thought is rendered back to us by the trumpets of the Last Judgment. Familiar as the voice of the mind is to each, the highest merit we ascribe to Moses, Plato, and Milton, is that they set at naught books and traditions, and spoke not what men did but what they thought. A man should learn to detect and watch that gleam of light which flashes across his mind from within, more than the luster of the firmament of bards and sages. Yet he dismisses without notice his thought, because it is his. In every work of genius we recognize our own rejected thoughts; they come back to us with a certain alienated majesty. Great works of art have no more affecting lesson for us than this. They teach us to abide by our spontaneous impression with good humored inflexibility then most when the whole cry of voices is on the other side. Else, tomorrow a stranger will say with masterly good sense precisely

Self-Reliance

Ralph Waldo Emerson

1   The other day I read some verses that contained some original and out-of-the-ordinary thoughts from a famous painter. Something pricks at the soul when it hears something original, no matter what the subject may be. The insight that one receives is more valuable than any thought that has been expressed. To believe your own thoughts, to believe that what is true for you in your private heart is true for all—that is genius. Speak your inner truth and it will be recognized as universal truth. The things that are inward always become outward, and our first thought is brought back to us by the trumpets of the last judgment. Though we are all familiar with the minds of Moses, Plato, and Milton, we hold them in the highest esteem because they defied books and traditions. They spoke about their thoughts, not just about men's deeds. We should learn to pay more attention to the flash of light that comes from within than to the dazzling light of poets and wise men. Instead, we often dismiss our thoughts simply because they are ours. In every work of genius we see our own discarded ideas. They come back to haunt us with a majesty that now belongs to someone else. Great works of art have only one lesson to teach us. Hang on to your first spontaneous thoughts with good-natured stubbornness. Hold on tighter when most people are on the other side. Otherwise, a stranger will say with great good sense

what we have thought and felt all the time, and we shall be forced to take with shame our own opinion from another. . . .

2   Trust thyself: every heart vibrates to that iron string. Accept the place the Divine Providence has found for you; the society of your contemporaries, the connection of events. Great men have always done so and confided themselves childlike to the genius of their age, betraying their perception that the Eternal was stirring at their heart, working through their hands, predominating in all their being. And we are now men, and must accept in the highest mind the same transcendent destiny; and not pinched in a corner, not cowards fleeing before a revolution, but redeemers and benefactors, pious aspirants to be noble clay plastic under the Almighty effort, let us advance and advance on Chaos and the Dark. . . .

3   The nonchalance of boys who are sure of a dinner and would disdain as much as a lord to do or say aught to conciliate one, is the healthy attitude of human nature. How is a boy the master of society; independent, irresponsible, looking out from his corner on such people and facts as pass by, he tries and sentences them on their merits, in the swift summary way of boys, as good, bad, interesting, silly, eloquent, troublesome. He cumbers himself never about consequences, about interests: he gives an independent, genuine verdict. You must court him: he does not court you. But the man is, as it were, clapping into jail by his consciousness. As soon as he has once acted or spoken with éclat, he is a committed person, watched by the sympathy or the hatred of hundreds whose affections must now enter into his account. There is no Lethe for this. Ah, that he could pass again into his neutral, godlike independence! . . .

tomorrow exactly what you have thought and known all along. Regrettably, you will be forced to take your own opinion from someone else. . . .

2   Trust yourself. Everyone knows in his heart that is the thing to do. Accept the role that Divine Providence has given you among the people and events of your time. Great men have always done this and have given their full trust to the genius of their age. They believed that the Eternal was touching their heart, working through their hands, controlling their being. Let us grow up and accept our great destiny. We must not be pushed into a corner in fear, nor run away from great change. Instead, we should be people who are noble clay and moldable in the hands of God, to serve and help others and stand against confusion and darkness. . . .

3   The boy who doesn't worry about where his next meal is coming from and wouldn't think of begging for it—that boy has a healthy attitude. He is the master of society: irresponsible but independent. He looks at people and facts as they pass by and quickly decides whether they are good, bad, interesting, silly, eloquent, or difficult. He doesn't worry about consequences or special interests. His views are independent and genuine. You must try to win him over; he will never attempt to win you over. But the grown person who becomes conscious of his thoughts becomes a prisoner of them. After he has acted or spoken in a particular way, he becomes committed to that way. He must now try to remain consistent for hundreds of people on both sides of the issue. Nothing he says is forgotten. If only he could return to that godlike time when he was an independent thinker!

4   Society everywhere is in conspiracy against the manhood of every one of its members. Society is a joint-stock company in which the members agree, for the better securing of his bread to each shareholder, to surrender the liberty and culture of the eater. The virtue in most request is conformity. Self-reliance is its aversion. It loves not realities and creators, but names and customs.

5   Whoso would be a man must be a nonconformist. He who would gather immortal palms must not be hindered by the name of goodness, but must explore if it be goodness. Nothing is at last sacred but the integrity of your own mind. Absolve you to yourself, and you shall have the suffrage of the world. I remember an answer which when quite young I was prompted to make to a valued adviser who was wont to importune me with the dear old doctrines of the church. On my saying, "What have I to do with the sacredness of traditions, if I live wholly from within?" my friend suggested—"But these impulses may be from below, not from above." I replied, "They do not seem to me to be such; but if I am the devil's child, I will live then from the devil." No law can be sacred to me but that of my nature. Good and bad are but names very readily transferable to that or this; the only right is what is after my constitution; the only wrong what is against it. A man is to carry himself in the presence of all opposition as if every thing were titular and ephemeral but he. I am ashamed to think how easily we capitulate to badges and names, to large societies and dead institutions. Every decent and well spoken individual affects and sways me more than is right. I ought to go upright and vital, and speak the rude truth in all ways. . . .

4   Society always tries to keep its members in line. Society is a company in which all the shareholders give up their individual freedom in order to have security together. The larger group prizes conformity, which is the opposite of self-reliance. It loves neither truth-tellers nor original thinkers. Instead, it loves etiquette and habits.

5   If you want to be a man, you must be a nonconformist. If you want to gain immortality for yourself, you must not be held back by some narrow idea of goodness. Indeed, you must explore goodness to see if it is, in fact, good. In the end, nothing is sacred except the integrity of your own mind. Free yourself from false guilt, and the whole world will support you. I remember an answer that I gave when I was quite young to a trusted adviser who wanted to tell me about the dear old traditions of the church. When I said, "Why do I need sacred traditions if I live my life from within?" my friend suggested, "But the impulses you feel may be evil instead of divine." I said, "I don't think these thoughts come from the devil, but if I am the devil's child, let me live like the devil." No law can be sacred to me except that of my own heart. Good and bad are only labels that can be easily transferred to this or that. The only right is what is in tune with my nature; the only wrong is what goes against it. When a man meets opposition, he should act as if nothing will endure except himself. I am ashamed at how easily we give in to name and rank, to so-called authorities, and their dead institutions. I am too easily influenced by decent people with smooth tongues. I should simply and clearly speak the awful truth at all times. . . .

6   What I must do, is all that concerns me, not what the people think. This rule, equally arduous in actual and in intellectual life, may serve for the whole distinction between greatness and meanness. It is the harder, because you will always find those who think they know what is your duty better than you know it. It is easy in the world to live after the world's opinion; it is easy in solitude to live after our own; but the great man is he who in the midst of the crowd keeps with perfect sweetness the independence of solitude.

7   The objection to conforming to usages that have become dead to you is, that it scatters your force. It loses your time and blurs the impression of your character. If you maintain a dead church, contribute to a dead Bible Society, vote with a great party either for the Government or against it, spread your table like base housekeepers—under all these screens I have difficulty to detect the precise man you are. And, of course, so much force is withdrawn from your proper life. But do your thing, and I shall know you. Do your work, and you shall reinforce yourself. . . .

8   The other terror that scares us from self-trust is our consistency; a reverence for our past act or word, because the eyes of others have no other data for computing our orbit than our past acts, and we are loath to disappoint them.

9   But why should you keep your head over your shoulder? Why drag about this corpse of your memory, lest you contradict somewhat you have stated in this or that public place? Suppose you should contradict yourself; what then? It seems to be a rule of wisdom never to rely on your memory alone, scarcely even in acts of pure memory, but to bring the past of judgment into the thousand-eye present, and live ever in a new day. . . .

6   I am concerned only with what I must do, not with what people think. This rule, difficult to follow in all aspects of life, helps distinguish between those who are great and those who are not. It becomes harder because you will always find people who think they know what your duty is better than you know it yourself. It is easy to live in the world if you go along with the crowd. It is easy to live according to your own beliefs if you live a life of solitude. But the great man is the one who keeps the independence of solitude in the middle of a crowd.

7   The problem with conforming to things you no longer believe in is that it scatters your energy. It wastes time and weakens your character. If you help maintain a dead church, give to a dead Bible Society, vote with a great party either for the government or against it—spreading out your favors in this way—it will be difficult to figure out who the exact person is under all these different masks. And so much energy is taken away from your real life. But do your own thing, and I will know you. Do your work, and you will strengthen yourself. . . .

8   The other fear that scares us away from trusting ourselves is consistency. We worship our past deeds or words because other people have no other way of figuring out the course of our lives except through our past actions, and we do not want to disappoint people.

9   But why should you keep looking over your shoulder at the past? Why drag around this corpse of your memory? Why worry about contradicting something you have said in this or that public place? What if you do contradict yourself? So what? Conventional wisdom says that you should be obsessed with the past and use it to judge every single thing that you do in the present. . . .

10   A foolish consistency is the hobgoblin of little minds, adored by little statesmen and philosophers and divines. With consistency, a great soul has simply nothing to do. He may as well concern himself with his shadow on the wall. Out upon your guarded lips! Sew them up with packthread, do. Else, if you would be a man, speak what you think today in words as hard as cannon balls, and tomorrow speak what tomorrow thinks in hard words again, though it contradict every thing you said today. Ah, then, exclaim the aged ladies, you shall be sure to be misunder-

11   stood. Misunderstood! It is a right fool's word. Is it so bad then to be misunderstood? Pythagoras was misunderstood, and Socrates, and Jesus, and Luther, and Copernicus, and Galileo, and Newton, and every pure and wise spirit that ever took flesh. To be great is to be misunderstood. . . .

12   I hope in these days we have heard the last of conformity and consistency. Let the words be

10   Small minds—afraid of the unknown—require consistency no matter what. Second-rate politicians, philosophers, and clergy adore consistency. Great souls, however, do not worry about consistency any more than they worry about their shadow on the wall. If you want to be consistent always, sew up your lips with twine. But if you want to be a man, speak what you think today in words as hard as cannonballs, and tomorrow speak what tomorrow thinks in hard words again, even if it contradicts everything you said today. Ah, then, the old ladies say, you are sure to be misunderstood.

11   Misunderstood! It is a stupid word. Is it so bad to be misunderstood? Pythagoras was misunderstood, and Socrates, and Jesus, and Luther, and Copernicus, and Galileo, and Newton, and every pure and wise spirit that ever lived. Great people are always misunderstood. . . .

Galileo Before the Inquisition

12   I hope we don't hear any more about conformity and consistency. Let these absurd words disappear

gazetted and ridiculous henceforward. Instead of the gong for dinner, let us hear a whistle from the Spartan fife. Let us never bow and apologize more. A great man is coming to eat at my house. I do not wish to please him: I wish that he should to please me. I will stand here for humanity, and though I would make it kind, I would make it true. Let us affront and reprimand the smooth mediocrity and squalid contentment of times, and hurl in the face of custom, and trade, and office, the fact which is the upshot of all history, that there is a great responsible Thinker and Actor working wherever a man works; that a true man belongs to no other time or place, but is the center of things. Where he is, there is nature. He measures you, and all men, and all events. . . . Every true man is a cause, a country, and an age; requires infinite spaces and numbers and time fully to accomplish his thought; and posterity seem to follow his steps as a procession. A man Caesar is born, and for ages after, we have a Roman Empire. Christ is born, and millions of minds so grow and cleave to his genius, that he is confounded with virtue and the possible of man. An institution is the lengthened shadow of one man . . . and all history resolves itself very easily into the biography of a few stout and earnest persons.

from our vocabulary. Instead of the dinner bell, let us hear a whistle from a Spartan fife. Let us stop bowing and apologizing. A well-known man is coming to eat at my house. I do not want to please him. I think he should want to please me. I represent humanity, and though I like to be polite, I must first of all be true. Let us confront and challenge everything in our age that is bland and ordinary and miserably content with itself. In the face of tradition and custom let us throw in the fact that there is a Power greater than ourselves working wherever a man works. A true man, an ideal individual, belongs to no time or place. He is at the center of all things. Where this individual is, there is the world. This person becomes the standard for all others and all events. . . . Every true man is a cause, a country, and an age. He requires unlimited space and time to fully accomplish his purpose, and the procession of history seems to follow in his footsteps. Caesar is born, and for years after, we have a Roman Empire. Christ is born, and millions of minds grow and cling to his genius, a genius that is imbued with goodness and all that is possible for man to be. An institution is only the long shadow of one man . . . and all history is only the biography of a few brave and sincere persons.

from Civil Disobedience

Henry David Thoreau

1   *I* heartily accept the motto, "That government is best which governs least"; and I should like to see it acted up to more rapidly and systematically. Carried out, it finally amounts to this, which also I believe—"that government is best which governs not at all"; and when men are prepared for it, that will be the kind of government which they will have. Government is at best but an expedient; but most governments are usually, and all governments are sometimes, inexpedient. The objections which have been brought against a standing army, and they are many and weighty, and deserve to prevail, may also at last be brought against a standing government. The standing army is only an arm of the standing government. The government itself, which is only the mode which the people have chosen to execute their will, is equally liable to be abused and perverted before the people can act through it. Witness the present Mexican war, the work of comparatively a few individuals using the standing government as their tool; for, in the outset, the people would not have consented to this measure. . . .

2   But, to speak practically and as a citizen, unlike those who call themselves no-government men, I ask

from Civil Disobedience

Henry David Thoreau

1   *I* completely agree with the saying, "The best government is the one that governs least." That is the kind of government I would like to see put into effect as soon as possible. If such a government were set up, it would be based on the following principle, which I also believe in: "The best government of all is the one that does not govern." When people are ready for it, that will be what they will have. Government at its best is a means to an end. Most governments, however, are no good at bringing about a desired end result. All governments fail to do so some of the time. The many, valid objections that have been raised against an army that is maintained in peacetime as well as in wartime may also be raised against a government that is maintained at all times. A permanent army is only an arm of a permanent government. Government is only the means for carrying out the will of the people, yet government is often misused before the people can act through it. Look at the present Mexican War. It is the work of a few individuals who used the government as their tool, for in the beginning the people would not have said yes to this war. . . .

2   Speaking in practical terms as a citizen (unlike those who are opposed to all government), I don't ask

for, not at once no government, but *at once* a better government. Let every man make known what kind of government would command his respect, and that will be one step toward obtaining it.

3   After all, the practical reason why, when the power is once in the hands of the people, a majority are permitted, and for a long period continue, to rule is not because they are most likely to be in the right, nor because this seems fairest to the minority, but because they are physically the strongest. But a government in which the majority rule in all cases cannot be based on justice, even as far as men understand it. Can there not be a government in which majorities do not virtually decide right and wrong, but conscience?—in which majorities decide only those questions to which the rule of expediency is applicable? Must the citizen ever for a moment, or in the least degree, resign his conscience to the legislator? Why has every man a conscience, then? I think that we should be men first, and subjects afterward. It is not desirable to cultivate a respect for the law, so much as for the right. The only obligation which I have a right to assume is to do at any time what I think right.

4   It is truly enough said that a corporation has no conscience; but a corporation of conscientious men is a corporation with a conscience. Law never made men a whit more just; and, by means of their respect for it, even the well-disposed are daily made the agents of injustice. A common and natural result of an undue respect for law is, that you may see a file of soldiers, colonel, captain, corporal, privates, powder-monkeys, and all, marching in admirable order over hill and dale to the wars, against their wills, ay, against their common sense and consciences, which

for the immediate end of government but for a better government immediately. Let every man speak out about the kind of government he could respect. That will be one step toward getting it.

3   After all, the practical reason why most people continue to rule is not because they are most likely to be right, nor because their rule seems fairest to the minority, but because they are the strongest physically. A government in which the majority rule all the time cannot be based on justice, however; that is understood. Is it possible to have a government that is not based on majority rule but on conscience? In this government, the majority would decide only those questions that have to do with self-interest. Must citizens always resign their consciences to the politicians? Why does every man have a conscience then? I think that we should be men first and subjects of a government second. It is not good to teach respect for the law above respect for what is right. The only duty that I have is to do what I think right at all times.

4   It is often said that a corporation has no conscience. However, a corporation of conscientious men is a corporation with conscience. The law has never made men one bit more just. In fact, even kind people become the carriers of injustice by their respect for law. The natural result of an unquestioning respect for law is a long line of soldiers, colonel, captain, corporal, privates, and boys carrying gunpowder marching in good order over hills and valleys to wars they don't believe in and don't support. This makes for very steep marching indeed; it causes the heart to

makes it very steep marching indeed, and produces a palpitation of the heart. They have no doubt that it is a damnable business in which they are concerned; they are all peaceably inclined. Now, what are they? Men at all? or small movable forts and magazines, at the service of some unscrupulous man in power? Visit the Navy Yard, and behold a marine, such a man as an American government can make, or such as it can make a man with its black arts—mere shadow and reminiscence of humanity, a man laid out alive and standing, and already, as one may say, buried under arms with funeral accompaniments, though it may be,

5   "Not a drum was heard, not a funeral note,
         As his corse to the rampart we hurried;
     Not a soldier discharged his farewell shot
         O'er the grave where our hero we buried."

6   The mass of men serve the state thus, not as men mainly, but as machines, with their bodies. They are the standing army, and the militia, jailers, constables, *posse comitatus,* etc. In most cases there is no free exercise whatever of the judgment or of the moral sense; but they put themselves on a level with wood and earth and stones; and wooden men can perhaps be manufactured that will serve the purpose as well. Such command no more respect than men of straw or a lump of dirt. They have the same sort of worth only as horses and dogs. Yet such as these even are commonly esteemed good citizens. Others—as most legislators, politicians, lawyers, ministers, and office-holders—serve the state chiefly with their heads; and, as they rarely make any moral distinctions, they are as likely to serve the devil, without *intending* it, as God. A very few—as heroes, patriots, martyrs, reformers in the great sense, and *men*—

pound. They know that what they are doing is horrible. They are, by nature, peace-loving. But what have they become? Men at all? Or small, movable military bases who serve some man in power who has no principles? Visit a dockyard and see a marine that the American government has made with its black magic—a mere shadow and memory of what it is to be human, a living dead man, prepared for war. Though alive, he is ready for war and for his own death, even if it only ends up like this:

5 "No drum was heard and no funeral note played,
As we raced with his corpse to the fort.
Not a soldier fired a farewell shot
On the grave where our hero was laid."

6 Most men serve the state not as men but as machines, with their bodies. They are the permanent army, and the citizens' army, the jailers, police, posses, etc. In most cases they have no freedom to make moral judgments. They are on the same level with wood and earth and stones. Wooden men can perhaps be manufactured that will serve the purpose as well. Such men get no more respect than men of straw or a lump of dirt. They are worth about as much as horses and dogs. Yet these kind of men are commonly considered good citizens. Others—legislators, politicians, lawyers, ministers, and officeholders—serve the state mostly with their heads. They rarely make any moral distinctions. They are as likely to serve the devil, without knowing it, as God. A very few—heroes, patriots, martyrs, social reformers, and others—serve the state with their consciences. For

serve the state with their consciences also, and so necessarily resist it for the most part; and they are commonly treated as enemies by it. . . .

7   Unjust laws exist: shall we be content to obey them, or shall we endeavor to amend them, and obey them until we have succeeded, or shall we transgress them at once? Men generally, under such a government as this, think that they ought to wait until they have persuaded the majority to alter them. They think that, if they should resist, the remedy would be worse than the evil. But it is the fault of the government itself that the remedy *is* worse than the evil. *It* makes it worse. Why is it not more apt to anticipate and provide for reform? Why does it not cherish its wise minority? Why does it cry and resist before it is hurt? Why does it not encourage its citizens to be on the alert to point out its faults, and *do* better than it would have them? Why does it always crucify Christ, and excommunicate Copernicus and Luther, and pronounce Washington and Franklin rebels? . . .

8   If the injustice is part of the necessary friction of the machine of government, let it go, let it go: perchance it will wear smooth—certainly the machine will wear out. If the injustice has a spring, or a pulley, or a rope, or a crank, exclusively for itself, then perhaps you may consider whether the remedy will not be worse than the evil; but if it is of such a nature that it requires you to be the agent of injustice to another, then, I say, break the law. Let your life be a counter-friction to stop the machine. What I have to do is to see, at any rate, that I do not lend myself to the wrong which I condemn. . . .

the most part they must resist the state, and they are commonly treated like enemies by the state. . . .

7   Unjust laws exist. Shall we happily obey them, or shall we try to change them and obey them until we have succeeded? Or shall we break them at once? Most men think that under our form of government they should wait until they have persuaded the majority to change the law. They think that if they resist, the remedy would be worse than the evil. But it is the government's fault that the remedy is worse than the evil. The government makes the remedy worse. Why isn't it better to think about these problems ahead of time and provide for reform? Why doesn't the government value its wise minority? Why does the government resist reform? Why doesn't it encourage its citizens to be alert and to point out its faults and do better? Why do governments always crucify Christ and excommunicate Copernicus and Luther and say that Washington and Franklin are rebels? . . .

8   If the injustice is simply like the necessary friction of the machine of government, let it go, let it go. Eventually, it will be worn smooth—certainly the machine will wear out. If the injustice has a spring, a pulley, a rope, or a crank exclusively for itself, then perhaps the remedy may be worse than the evil. But if the evil is of the kind that makes one person hurt another human being, then I say, break the law. Use your life to stop the machine. What I have to do is to make sure that I do not become a part of the wrong which I condemn. . . .

9   I meet this American government, or its representative, the State government, directly, and face to face,
once a year—no more—in the person of its tax-gatherer; this is the only mode in which a man situated as I
am necessarily meets it; and it then says distinctly,
Recognize me; and the simplest, the most effectual,
and, in the present posture of affairs, the indispens-
ablest mode of treating with it on this head, of
expressing your little satisfaction with and love for it,
is to deny it then. My civil neighbor, the tax-gatherer, is
the very man I have to deal with—for it is, after all,
with men and not with parchment that I quarrel—and
he has voluntarily chosen to be an agent of the government. How shall he ever know well what he is and
does as an officer of the government, or as a man, until
he is obliged to consider whether he shall treat me, his
neighbor, for whom he has respect, as a neighbor and
well-disposed man, or as a maniac and disturber of the
peace, and see if he can get over this obstruction to his
neighborliness without a ruder and more impetuous
thought or speech corresponding with his action. I
know this well, that if one thousand, if one hundred, if
ten men whom I could name—if ten *honest* men only—
ay, if *one* HONEST man, in this State of
Massachusetts, *ceasing to hold slaves,* were actually to
withdraw from this copartnership, and be locked up in
the county jail therefore, it would be the abolition of
slavery in America. For it matters not how small the
beginning may seem to be: what is once well done is
done forever. But we love better to talk about it: that
we say is our mission. Reform keeps many scores of
newspapers in its service, but not one man. . . .

10   Under a government which imprisons any
unjustly, the true place for a just man is also a
prison. The proper place today, the only place which
Massachusetts has provided for her freer and less

9 I meet this American government, or its representative, the state government, face to face once a year—no more—when I meet the tax collector. This is the only way in which a man such as myself meets the government. It then says to me, "Recognize me." The simplest, most effective, and in the present state of affairs, the very best way of dealing with it and expressing your feelings about it, is to just say no. My neighbor, the tax collector, is the man I have to deal with, for it is with men, not with pieces of paper, that I quarrel. He has chosen of his own free will to represent the state. How will he ever understand what he does as an officer of the government unless as a man he has to think about how to treat me, a neighbor that he respects and likes? Shall he treat me as a friendly neighbor or as a maniac and disturber of the peace? How will he be able to carry out his job and handle this obstacle to our relationship without being rude? I am sure of this: if 1,000, if 100, if I could name 10 men—if 10 *honest* men only—yes, if 1 HONEST man, in this state of Massachusetts, stopped holding slaves and actually withdrew from this system and got locked up in the county jail, then it would be the end of slavery in America. For it does not matter how small the beginning may be. What is once well done is done forever. But we would rather talk about it; we say that is our mission. Reform keeps dozens of newspapers busy, but not one man. . . .

10 Under a government that imprisons anyone unjustly, the only place for a just man is in prison. The only place that Massachusetts has provided for her freer and less hopeless spirits is in her prisons.

desponding spirits, is in her prisons, to be put out and locked out of the State by her own act, as they have already put themselves out by their principles. It is there that the fugitive slave, and the Mexican prisoner on parole, and the Indian come to plead the wrongs of his race should find them; on that separate, but more free and honorable, ground, where the State places those who are not *with* her, but *against* her—the only house in a slave State in which a free man can abide with honor. If any think that their influence would be lost there, and their voices no longer afflict the ear of the State, that they would not be as an enemy within its walls, they do not know by how much truth is stronger than error, nor how much more eloquently and effectively he can combat injustice who has experienced a little in his own person. Cast your whole vote, not a strip of paper merely, but your whole influence. A minority is powerless while it conforms to the majority; it is not even a minority then; but it is irresistible when it clogs by its whole weight. If the alternative is to keep all just men in prison, or give up war and slavery, the State will not hesitate which to choose.

11   If a thousand men were not to pay their tax bills this year, that would not be a violent and bloody measure, as it would be to pay them, and enable the State to commit violence and shed innocent blood. This is, in fact, the definition of a peaceable revolution, if any such is possible. If the tax-gatherer, or any other public officer, asks me, as one has done, "But what shall I do?" my answer is, "If you really wish to do anything, resign your office." When the subject has refused allegiance, and the officer has resigned his office, then the revolution is accomplished. But even suppose blood should flow. Is there not a sort of blood shed when the conscience is

Here they will be locked out of the government just as they have already locked themselves out by their own principles. Here the fugitive slave, the Mexican prisoner on parole, and the Indian come to present their case against the wrongs that have been committed against them. The only house in which a free man in a slave state can stay with honor is in prison. If anyone thinks that his influence would be lost in prison, and that his voice would no longer be heard by the government, that they would not be effective in prison, they are wrong. They do not know how much stronger truth is than error, nor how much more eloquent and effective a person can be who has experienced a little injustice in his own life. Cast your whole vote. Don't just vote on a piece of paper. Use all your influence. A minority that conforms to the majority is powerless. It is not even a minority. But if a minority clogs up the works with its own weight, it cannot be stopped. If the alternative is to keep all just men in prison or to give up war and slavery, the government will not hesitate which to choose.

11   If 1,000 men did not pay their tax bills this year, that would be less violent and bloody than if they paid those bills and in so doing enabled the government to kill and commit acts of violence. This is, in fact, the definition of a peaceable revolution, if such a thing is possible. If the tax collector or any other public official asks me as one has done, "But what shall I do?" my answer is, "If you really want to do something, resign your job." When a citizen refuses to support a cause, and the official resigns his office, then the revolution is over. But suppose blood should flow. Is there not some sort of blood shed when the conscience is wounded? A man's true manhood and

wounded? Through this wound a man's real manhood and immortality flow out, and he bleeds to an ever-lasting death. I see this blood flowing now. . . .

12   I have paid no poll tax for six years. I was put into a jail once on this account, for one night; and, as I stood considering the walls of solid stone, two or three feet thick, the door of wood and iron, a foot thick, and the iron grating which strained the light, I could not help being struck with the foolishness of that institution which treated me as if I were mere flesh and blood and bones, to be locked up. I won-dered that it should have concluded at length that this was the best use it could put me to, and had never thought to avail itself of my services in some way. I saw that, if there was a wall of stone between me and my townsmen, there was a still more difficult one to climb or break through before they could get to be as free as I was. I did not for a moment feel confined, and the walls seemed a great waste of stone and mortar. I felt as if I alone of all my townsmen had paid my tax.

13   They plainly did not know how to treat me, but behaved like persons who are underbred. In every threat and in every compliment there was a blunder; for they thought that my chief desire was to stand on the other side of that stone wall. I could not but smile to see how industriously they locked the door on my meditations, which followed them out again without let or hindrance, and *they* were really all that was dangerous. As they could not reach me, they had resolved to punish my body; just as boys, if they cannot come at some person against whom they have a spite, will abuse his dog. I saw that the State was half-witted, that it was timid as a lone woman with

everlasting life flow out, and he bleeds an everlasting death. I see this blood flowing now. . . .

12   I have not paid poll tax for six years. I was put into a jail once for that reason for one night. As I stood observing the walls of solid stone, two or three feet thick, the door of wood and iron, a foot thick, and the iron grating which strained the light, I could not help being struck with the foolishness of an institution that treated me as if I were only flesh and blood and bones, to be locked up. I wondered why it thought that this was the best use it could put me to, and never thought to use my services in some way. I saw that, if there was a wall of stone between me and my townsmen, there was a still more difficult wall to climb or break through before they could become as free as I was. I did not for a moment feel locked up, and the walls seemed a great waste of stone and mortar. I felt as if I was the only townsman who had paid my tax.

13   They obviously did not know how to treat me but clearly showed their bad manners. With every threat and every compliment they implied that my chief wish was to stand on the other side of that stone wall, which was not true at all. I could not help but smile to see how carefully they locked the door on my thoughts, which followed them out again without hindrance. The only danger lay in these men. Because they could not reach me, they had decided to punish my body just like boys who hold a grudge against someone and get even by hurting his dog. I saw that the government was idiotic, that it was as timid as a lonely woman with her silver spoons, and

her silver spoons, and that it did not know its friends from its foes, and I lost all my remaining respect for it, and pitied it.

14   Thus the State never intentionally confronts a man's sense, intellectual or moral, but only his body, his senses. It is not armed with superior wit or honesty, but with superior physical strength. I was not born to be forced. I will breathe after my own fashion. Let us see who is the strongest. What force has a multitude? They only can force me who obey a higher law than I. They force me to become like themselves. I do not hear of *men* being *forced* to live this way or that by masses of men. What sort of life were that to live? When I meet a government which says to me, "Your money or your life," why should I be in haste to give it my money? It may be in a great strait, and not know what to do: I cannot help that. It must help itself; do as I do. It is not worth the while to snivel about it. I am not responsible for the successful working of the machinery of society. I am not the son of the engineer.

15   I perceive that, when an acorn and a chestnut fall side by side, the one does not remain inert to make way for the other, but both obey their own laws, and spring and grow and flourish as best they can, till one, perchance, overshadows and destroys the other. If a plant cannot live according to its nature, it dies; and so a man.

that it did not know its friends from its enemies. I lost all my remaining respect for government and pitied it.

14   Thus the government never intentionally confronts a man's intelligence or morals but only his physical senses. It is not armed with superior reasoning or honesty but with superior physical strength. I was not born to be forced. I will breathe in my own way. Let us see who is the strongest. What force has the most power? No one has power over me except those who obey a higher law than I do. They force me to become like themselves. I do not hear of *men* being *forced* to live this way or that by masses of men. What sort of life would that be? When I meet a government which says to me, "Your money or your life," why should I be in a hurry to give it my money? It may be in a difficult spot and not know what to do. I cannot help that. It must help itself and do as I do. It is not worthwhile to fret about it. I am not responsible for the successful workings of the machinery of society. I am not the son of the engineer.

15   I see that, when an acorn and a chestnut fall side by side, the one does not remain lifeless to make way for the other but both obey their own laws and sprout and grow and flourish as best they can, until one, maybe, overshadows and destroys the other. If a plant cannot live according to its nature, it dies; and so a man.

from Walden

Henry David Thoreau

1   When I first took up my abode in the woods, that is, began to spend my nights as well as days there, which, by accident, was on Independence Day, or the fourth of July, 1845, my house was not finished for winter, but was merely a defense against the rain, without plastering or chimney, the walls being of rough weather-stained boards, with wide chinks, which made it cool at night. The upright white hewn studs and freshly planed door and window casings gave it a clean and airy look, especially in the morning, when its timbers were saturated with dew, so that I fancied that by noon some sweet gum would exude from them.

2   To my imagination it retained through the day more or less of this auroral character, reminding me of a certain house on a mountain which I had visited a year before. This was an airy and unplastered cabin, fit to entertain a traveling god, and where a goddess might trail her garments. The winds which passed over my dwelling were such as sweep over the ridges of mountains, bearing the broken strains, or celestial parts only, of terrestrial music. The morning wind forever blows, the poem of creation is uninterrupted; but few are the ears that hear it. Olympus is but the outside of the earth everywhere. . . .

3   I was seated by the shore of a small pond, about a mile and a half south of the village of Concord and

from Walden

Henry David Thoreau

1 When I first went to my home in the woods and began to spend my nights as well as my days there—which was, by accident, on Independence Day, or the Fourth of July, 1845—my house was not finished for the winter. The house was at that time only a shelter against the rain with no plastering or chimney and with walls that were made of rough weather-stained boards with wide cracks, which made it cool at night. The upright boards, newly smoothed door, and window frames gave it a clean and airy look, especially in the morning, when the wood was so soaked with dew that I imagined that by noon the boards would be oozing sweet gum.

2 In my imagination the house kept its dawn-like quality throughout the day. This house reminded me of another house on a mountain which I had visited a year before. That place was a simple, open cabin—perfect for entertaining a traveling god or a goddess whose robes flowed behind her. The winds that passed over my cabin were like the ones that sweep the ridges of mountains, but these winds carried only the heavenly parts of earth's music. The morning wind blows forever. You can always hear the poem of creation, but few people do. The home of the gods is the outside of the earth, everywhere. . . .

3 I was sitting on the shore of a small pond that was on slightly higher ground than the town of

somewhat higher than it, in the midst of an extensive wood between that town and Lincoln, and about two miles south of that our only field known to fame, Concord Battle Ground; but I was so low in the woods that the opposite shore, half a mile off, like the rest, covered with wood, was my most distant horizon. For the first week, whenever I looked out on the pond it impressed me like a tarn high up on the side of a mountain, its bottom far above the surface of other lakes, and, as the sun arose, I saw it throwing off its nightly clothing of mist, and here and there, by degrees, its soft ripples or its smooth reflecting surface was revealed, while the mists, like ghosts, were stealthily withdrawing in every direction into the woods, as at the breaking up of some nocturnal conventicle. The very dew seemed to hang upon the trees later into the day than usual, as on the sides of mountains.

4   This small lake was of most value as a neighbor in the intervals of a gentle rainstorm in August, when, both air and water being perfectly still, but the sky overcast, mid-afternoon had all the serenity of evening, and the wood thrush sang around, and was heard from shore to shore. A lake like this is never smoother than at such a time; and the clear portion of the air above it being shallow and darkened by clouds, the water, full of light and reflections, becomes a lower heaven itself so much the more important.

5   From a hilltop nearby, where the wood had been recently cut off, there was a pleasing vista southward across the pond, through a wide indentation in the hills which form the shore there, where their opposite sides sloping toward each other suggested a stream flowing out in that direction through a wooded valley, but stream there was none. That way I

Concord and about a mile and a half south. I was in the middle of a large woods between Concord and Lincoln and about two miles south of our only famous field, Concord Battleground. I was, however, in such a low spot in the woods that the farthest I could see was the opposite shore, half a mile off, also wooded. Whenever I looked out on the pond during the first week, the pond looked to me like a small lake high up on a mountain whose bottom was far higher than the surface of other lakes. As the sun rose, I saw mists rising from the pond. Little by little I saw the soft ripples on the pond's smooth reflecting surface. The mists withdrew in snakelike fashion in every direction into the woods like the breaking up of some evening meeting of ghosts. Even the dew seemed to hang on the trees later into the day than usual, as it does on the sides of mountains.

4   I appreciated this small lake the most in between August rainstorms when both the air and the water were perfectly still. When the sky was overcast in the mid-afternoon, and the wood thrush sang across the shores of the lake, it was as peaceful as evening. A lake like this is never smoother than at such times. The air above the lake is clear and shallow and darkened by clouds. The water below is full of light and reflections. It becomes like a lower heaven.

5   From a nearby hilltop of recently cut woods, there was a pleasant view south across the pond. A wide cut in the hills and the sloping sides might make you think a stream is there, but that isn't the case. In that direction I looked between and over the near green hills to some distant and higher ones in the horizon that were tinted blue. Indeed, by standing on

looked between and over the near green hills to some distant and higher ones in the horizon, tinged with blue. Indeed, by standing on tiptoe I could catch a glimpse of some of the peaks of the still bluer and more distant mountain ranges in the northwest, those true-blue coins from heaven's own mint, and also of some portion of the village. But in other directions, even from this point, I could not see over or beyond the woods which surrounded me.

6   It is well to have some water in your neighborhood, to give buoyancy to and float the earth. One value even of the smallest well is, that when you look into it you see that earth is not continent but insular. This is as important as that it keeps butter cool. When I looked across the pond from this peak toward the Sudbury meadows, which in time of flood I distinguished elevated perhaps by a mirage in their seething valley, like a coin in a basin, all the earth beyond the pond appeared like a thin crust insulated and floated even by this small sheet of intervening water, and I was reminded that this on which I dwelt was but dry land. . . .

7   Every morning was a cheerful invitation to make my life of equal simplicity, and I may say innocence, with Nature herself. I have been as sincere a worshipper of Aurora as the Greeks. I got up early and bathed in the pond; that was a religious exercise, and one of the best things which I did. They say that characters were engraven on the bathing tub of king Tching-thang to this effect: "Renew thyself completely each day; do it again, and again, and forever again." I can understand that. Morning brings back the heroic ages. I was as much affected by the faint hum of a mosquito making its invisible and unimaginable tour through my apartment at earliest dawn,

tiptoe, I could catch a glimpse of some of the peaks of the still bluer and more distant mountain ranges in the northwest and also some parts of the town. Those mountains were the true-blue coins from heaven's own mint. But in other directions, even from this point, I could not see over or beyond the woods which surrounded me.

6   It is good to have some water in your neighborhood, to keep that part of the earth afloat. One value of even the smallest well is that when you look into it you see that the earth is made up of islands. This is as important as the fact that water keeps butter cool. I looked across the pond from this peak toward the Sudbury meadows. When the meadows flood, they seem to be higher. Perhaps this is a mirage, like looking at a coin in a basin. All the earth beyond the pond looked like a thin crust set apart and held up by this small piece of water that comes in between us. I was reminded that what I live on is only dry land. . . .

7   Every morning was a cheerful invitation to be as simple and innocent as Nature herself. I have been as sincere a worshipper of sunrise as the Greeks were. I got up early and bathed in the pond. That was a spiritual exercise, and one of the best things that I did. They say that writing was engraved on the bathtub of King Tching-thang that said: "Renew yourself completely each day. Do it again and again and forever again." I understand that. Morning makes you feel like a hero. While I was sitting there at dawn with the door and windows open, I was as fascinated by the faint hum of a mosquito flying around my apartment as I would have been by a

when I was sitting with door and windows open, as I could be by any trumpet that ever sang of fame. It was Homer's requiem; itself an *Iliad* and *Odyssey* in the air, singing its own wrath and wanderings. There was something cosmical about it; a standing advertisement, till forbidden, of the everlasting vigor and fertility of the world.

8   The morning, which is the most memorable season of the day, is the awakening hour. Then there is least somnolence in us; and for an hour, at least, some part of us awakes which slumbers all the rest of the day and night. Little is to be expected of that day, if it can be called a day, to which we are not awakened by our Genius, but by the mechanical nudgings of some servitor, are not awakened by our own newly acquired force and aspirations from within, accompanied by the undulations of celestial music, instead of factory bells, and a fragrance filling the air—to a higher life than we fell asleep from; and thus the darkness bear its fruit, and prove itself to be good, no less than the light. That man who does not believe that each day contains an earlier, more sacred, and auroral hour than he has yet profaned, has despaired of life, and is pursuing a descending and darkening way. After a partial cessation of his sensuous life, the soul of man, or its organs rather, are reinvigorated each day, and his Genius tries again what noble life it can make.

9   All memorable events, I should say, transpire in morning time and in a morning atmosphere. The Vedas say, "All intelligences awake with the morning." Poetry and art, and the fairest and most memorable of the actions of men, date from such an hour. All poets and heroes, like Memnon, are the children of Aurora, and emit their music at sunrise. To him

trumpet singing about fame. The mosquito was singing its own version of the *Iliad* and the *Odyssey*—heroic songs of all that had happened to it in its wanderings on earth. There was something about the mosquito that seemed to represent the whole world. In some way it symbolized the everlasting energy and fertility of the world.

8   The best time of day is the morning, the awakening hour. At that time we have the least amount of sleep in us. For an hour, at least, some part of us wakes up which has slept the rest of the day and night. You can't expect very much from a day in which a clock wakes you up instead of your own mind. Instead of factory bells, your inner power and ambition should awaken you along with the sweet smells and heavenly music of nature. These things awaken us to a higher life than what we fell asleep from. Thus, the darkness bears fruit and proves itself no less good than the light. The man who does not believe that each day contains an earlier, more sacred hour than he has yet experienced, has given up on life and is on a downward spiral. After sleep, the soul of man, or at least his internal organs, are renewed daily. His intelligence tries once again to make life noble.

9   Everything that is important takes place in the morning and in a morning atmosphere. The ancient Hindu scriptures say, "All intelligence awakes with the morning." Poetry, art, and all the best actions of men occur in the early morning. All poets and heroes, like Memnon, are children of the dawn. They create their best works at sunrise. To the person who keeps

whose elastic and vigorous thought keeps pace with the sun, the day is a perpetual morning. It matters not what the clocks say or the attitudes and labors of men. Morning is when I am awake and there is a dawn in me. Moral reform is the effort to throw off sleep. Why it is that men give so poor an account of their day if they have not been slumbering? They are not such poor calculators. If they had not been overcome with drowsiness they would have performed something. The millions are awake enough for physical labor; but only one in a million is awake enough for effective intellectual exertion, only one in a hundred million to a poetic or divine life. To be awake is to be alive. I have never yet met a man who was quite awake. How could I have looked him in the face?

10   We must learn to reawaken and keep ourselves awake, not by mechanical aids, but by an infinite expectation of the dawn, which does not forsake us in our soundest sleep. I know of no more encouraging fact than the unquestionable ability of man to elevate his life by a conscious endeavor. It is something to be able to paint a particular picture, or to carve a statue, and so to make a few objects beautiful; but it is far more glorious to carve and paint the very atmosphere and medium through which we look, which morally we can do. To affect the quality of the day, that is the highest of arts. Every man is tasked to make his life, even in its details, worthy of the contemplation of his most elevated and critical hour. If we refused, or rather used up, such paltry information as we get, the oracles would distinctly inform us how this might be done.

11   I went to the woods because I wished to live deliberately, to front only the essential facts of life, and see if I could not learn what it had to teach, and not,

his thoughts flexible and vigorous throughout the day, every part of the day is morning. It doesn't matter what the clocks say, or what other men say or do. Morning is when I am awake, and the dawn is in me. To change society we must be wide awake. Why is it that men speak so poorly about a day in which they have not slept? They are not stupid. They know that if they had not been so tired all day, they might have accomplished something. Millions of people are awake enough for physical work, but only one in a million is alert enough to do intellectual work. Only one in a hundred million rises to a poetic or a divine life. To be awake is to be alive. I have never yet met a man who was fully awake. How could I have looked him in the face?

10   We must learn to wake up and to keep ourselves awake, not artificially, but by always expecting the dawn. This dawn is always within us, even in our deepest sleep. The most encouraging fact is that a man can raise his life to a higher plane by becoming fully conscious of what he is doing. It is one thing to paint a picture or carve a statue and thus to make a few beautiful objects. But it is far more glorious to adorn the very day itself, which morally we can do. To change the quality of the day—that is the highest art form. Every man's challenge is to make his life, even in its details, worthy of his most intense self-criticism. If we can't learn through self-criticism, then we must turn to the wisdom of the ages for help.

11   I went to the woods because I wanted to live a life of meaning and purpose. I wanted to face the essence of life and see if I could learn what life had to teach,

12   when I came to die, discover that I had not lived. I did not wish to live what was not life, living is so dear; nor did I wish to practice resignation, unless it was quite necessary. I wanted to live deep and suck out all the marrow of life, to live so sturdily and Spartanlike as to put to rout all that was not life, to cut a broad swath and shave close, to drive life into a corner, and reduce it to its lowest terms, and, if it proved to be mean, why then to get the whole and genuine meanness of it, and publish its meanness to the world; or if it were sublime, to know it by experience, and be able to give a true account of it in my next excursion. For most men, it appears to me, are in a strange uncertainty about it, whether it is of the devil or of God, and have somewhat hastily concluded that it is the chief end of man here to "glorify God and enjoy him forever."

13   Still we live meanly, like ants, though the fable tells us that we were long ago changed into men; like pygmies we fight with cranes; it is error upon error, and clout upon clout, and our best virtue has for its occasion a superfluous and evitable wretchedness. Our life is frittered away by detail. An honest man has hardly need to count more than his ten fingers, or in extreme cases he may add his ten toes, and lump the rest. Simplicity, simplicity, simplicity! I say, let your affairs be as two or three, and not a hundred or a thousand; instead of a million count half a dozen, and keep your accounts on your thumbnail. In the midst of this chopping sea of civilized life, such are the clouds and storms and quicksands and thousand and one items to be allowed for, that a man has to live, if he would not founder and go to the bottom and not make his port at all, by dead reckoning, and he must be a great calculator indeed who succeeds. Simplify, simplify. Instead of three

12 and not, when I died, discover that I had not lived. I did not want to live anything that was not really life because living is so precious. Nor did I want to give in or give up unless it was absolutely necessary. I wanted to live deep and suck out the marrow of life, to live so vigorously and so simply as to chase out everything that was not really life, to cut a broad path and shave close. I wanted to drive life into a corner and reduce it to its lowest terms, and if it proved to be empty, why then to get the absolute and genuine emptiness out of it and to tell the world. Or if it were divine, to know by experience and to write the truth about it in my next visit. For most men, it seems to me, don't know whether life is controlled by the devil or by God. Without really thinking about it, they say that the purpose of man on earth is to "glorify God and enjoy him forever."

13 So we live unimportant lives, like ants, though the fable tells us that we became men long ago. Like pygmies we fight with cranes.[1] We lay one mistake over another, and one patch over another. The best things that we do are in response to misery that we could have easily avoided in the first place. Our life is wasted in little details. An honest man doesn't need to count more than his ten fingers, or in extreme cases, he may add his ten toes, and forget the rest. Simplicity, simplicity, simplicity! I tell you, keep your business limited to two or three things, not a hundred or a thousand. Instead of a million things, have six, and keep your records on your thumbnail. In the middle of this short and perilous life, there are many clouds and storms and quicksands and a thousand and one items to keep track of. A man who doesn't want to stumble and fall to the bottom, a man

---

1 **Like pygmies . . . cranes:** This is a reference to a story told by Homer in the *Iliad*. In the story the pygmies were so small that they were frightened by cranes.

14   meals a day, if it be necessary eat but one; instead of
      a hundred dishes, five; and reduce other things in
      proportion. . . .

15   Why should we live with such hurry and waste of
      life? We are determined to be starved before we are
      hungry. Men say that a stitch in time saves nine, and
      so they take a thousand stitches today to save nine
      tomorrow. As for work, we haven't any of any conse-
      quence. We have the Saint Vitus' dance, and cannot
      possibly keep our heads still. If I should only give a
      few pulls at the parish bell rope, for a fire, that is,
      without setting the bell, there is hardly a man on his
      farm in the outskirts of Concord, notwithstanding
      that press of engagements which was his excuse so
      many times this morning, nor a boy, nor a woman, I
      might almost say, but would forsake all and follow
      that sound, not mainly to save property from the
      flames, but, if we will confess the truth, much more
      to see it burn, since burn it must, and we, be it
      known did not set it on fire—or to see it put out, and
      have a hand in it, if that is done as handsomely; yes,
      even if it were the parish church itself.

16   Hardly a man takes a half hour's nap after din-
      ner, but when he wakes he holds up his head and
      asks, "What's the news?" as if the rest of mankind
      had stood his sentinels. Some give directions to be
      waked every half hour, doubtless for no other pur-
      pose; and then, to pay for it, they tell what they have
      dreamed. After a night's sleep the news is as indis-
      pensable as the breakfast. "Pray tell me anything
      new that has happened to a man anywhere on this
      globe," and he reads it over his coffee and rolls, that a
      man has had his eyes gouged out this morning on the

14   who succeeds in reaching port, must be able to calculate accurately and have a great head for numbers. Simplify, simplify. Instead of three meals a day, eat one. Instead of a hundred dishes, use five. Reduce other things in proportion to that. . . .

15   Why do we hurry and waste our lives? We try to starve ourselves before we are even hungry. Men say that a stitch in time saves nine, and so they take a thousand stitches today to save nine tomorrow. As for work, we don't have any that really matters. We have the Saint Vitus' dance[2] and cannot keep our heads still. If I rang the parish bell for a fire, every farmer on the outskirts of Concord (even the one who excused himself this morning because of a long list of appointments), as well as every boy or woman, would want to drop everything and follow that sound. The main reason, to be truthful, is not that they want to save property from burning up. They're more interested in seeing it burn, since burn it must and we did not set it on fire—or to see it put out, and to help with that if that is done as well. Yes, that would be true even if it were the parish church itself.

16   There is hardly a man who doesn't take a half hour's nap after dinner, wake up, lift his head, and ask, "What's the news?" as if the rest of mankind had stood watch while he slept. Some ask to be awakened every half hour, probably for no other purpose; and then to pay for it, they tell us what they have dreamed. After an entire night's sleep the news is almost as important as breakfast itself. "Please tell me anything new that has happened to any man anywhere on earth." Over coffee and rolls he reads

2 **Saint Vitus' dance:** nervous disease that is characterized by rapid jerky movements of the body

Wachito River; never dreaming the while that he lives in the dark unfathomed mammoth cave of this world, and has but the rudiment of an eye himself.

17   For my part, I could easily do without the post office. I think that there are very few important communications made through it. To speak critically, I never received more than one or two letters in my life—I wrote this some years ago—that were worth the postage. The penny post is, commonly, an institution through which you seriously offer a man that penny for his thoughts which is so often safely offered in jest. And I am sure that I never read any memorable news in a newspaper. If we read of one man robbed, or murdered, or killed by accident, or one house burned, or one vessel wrecked, or one steamboat blown up, or one cow run over on the Western Railroad, or one mad dog killed, or one lot of grasshoppers in the winter, we never need read of another. One is enough. . . .

18   Let us spend one day as deliberately as Nature, and not be thrown off the track by every nutshell and mosquito's wing that falls on the rails. Let us rise early and fast, or break fast, gently and without perturbation; let company come and let company go, let the bells ring and the children cry, determined to make a day of it. Why should we knock under and go with the stream? Let us not be upset and overwhelmed in that terrible rapid and whirlpool called a dinner, situated in the meridian shallows. Weather this danger and you are safe, for the rest of the way is downhill. With unrelaxed nerves, with morning vigor, sail by it, looking another way, tied to the mast like Ulysses. If the engine whistles, let it whistle till it is hoarse for its pains. If the

that a man has had his eyes gouged out this morning on the Wachito River. At the same time he never realizes that he himself lives in a huge dark cave of this world and that he actually sees very little.

17   If it were up to me, I could easily do without the post office. I think that very little of importance is said through it. Looked at critically, I never received more than one or two letters in my life—I wrote this some years ago—that were worth the postage. A penny letter is, most often, just a way in which you actually give a man that penny for his thoughts that we joke about. And I am sure that I never read any important news in a newspaper. If we read of one man robbed or murdered or killed by accident or one house burned, or one ship wrecked, or one steamboat blown up, or one cow run over on the Western Railroad, or one mad dog killed, or one lot of grasshoppers in the winter, we never need to read of another. One is enough. . . .

18   Let us spend one day as unhurried as Nature does and not be thrown off by every nutshell or mosquito's wing that falls upon the track. Let us rise early and quickly or eat our breakfast quietly and without interruption. Let company come and go, let the bells ring, and the children cry. Be determined to make a day of it. Why should we knuckle under and go along with things as they are? Don't allow yourself to be upset and overwhelmed by the pull and force of something at noonday called dinner. If you can get through this danger, you are safe, for the rest of the way is downhill. With steely nerves, with morning vigor, sail by noontime, looking another way, tied to the mast like Ulysses.[3] If the engine whistles,

3 **Ulysses:** The King of Ithaca and Greek leader in the Trojan War who reached home after wandering for ten years. At one point he tied himself to the ship's mast so he could hear, but not be tempted by, the seductive song of the sirens.

bell rings, why should we run? We will consider what kind of music they are like.

19   Let us settle ourselves, and work and wedge our feet downward through the mud and slush of opinion, and prejudice, and tradition, and delusion, and appearance, that alluvion which covers the globe, through Paris and London, through New York and Boston and Concord, through church and state, through poetry and philosophy and religion, till we come to a hard bottom and rocks in place, which we can call reality, and say, This is, and no mistake; and then begin, have a *point d'appui,* below freshet and frost and fire, a place where you might found a wall or a state, or set a lamppost safely or perhaps a gauge, not a Nilometer, but a Realometer, that future ages might know how deep a freshet of shams and appearances had gathered from time to time. If you stand right fronting and face to face a fact, you will see the sun glimmer on both its surfaces, as if it were a cimeter, and feel its sweet edge dividing you through the heart and marrow, and so you will happily conclude your mortal career. Be it life or death, we crave only reality. If we are really dying, let us hear the rattle in our throats and feel cold in the extremities; if we are alive, let us go about our business.

20   Time is but the stream I go a-fishing in. I drink at it; but while I drink I see the sandy bottom and detect how shallow it is. Its thin current slides away, but eternity remains, I would drink deeper; fish in the sky, whose bottom is pebbly with stars. I cannot count one; I know not the first letter of the alphabet. I have always been regretting that I was not as wise as the day I was born. The intellect is a cleaver; it discerns and rifts its way into the secret of things. I do not wish to be any more busy with my hands than

let it whistle till it is hoarse. If the bell rings, why should we run? Think about what kind of music it is.

19   Let us settle ourselves and work and wedge our feet downward through the mud and slush of public opinion, prejudice, tradition, delusion, and appearances. All of these flood the earth from Paris and London to New York, Boston, and Concord. They seep into church and state affairs, through poetry, philosophy, and religion. Finally, we will come to a hard bottom with rocks in place that we can call reality. Make no mistake about it, this is our base. It is below streams, frost, and fire. It is a place where you might pour a wall, found a country, or set a lamppost safely. You could set a depth-gauge here, not to measure the depth of a river but to measure reality so that future ages might know how deep the stream of sham and appearance was from time to time. If you face a fact squarely, you will see the sun shining on both its surfaces, as if it were a blade. You will feel its sweet edge dividing you through the heart and bone, and so you will happily die. In life or in death, we crave only reality. If we are really dying, let us hear the rattle in our throats and feel the cold growing in our arms and legs. If we are alive, let us go about our business.

20   Time is only the stream I fish in. When I drink I see how shallow the sandy bottom is. Its current slides away. Eternity remains. I would like to drink deeper and to fish in the sky whose bottom is pebbled with stars. I cannot count to one. I do not know the first letter of the alphabet. I regret that I am not as wise as the day I was born. The mind is a sharp-edged butcher's knife. It cracks open the secret of things. I do not want to be any more busy with my hands than necessary. My head is my hands and feet.

is necessary. My head is hands and feet. I feel all my best faculties concentrated in it. My instinct tells me that my head is an organ for burrowing, as some creatures use their snout and forepaws, and with it I would mine and burrow my way through these hills. I think that the richest vein is somewhere here-abouts; so by the divining rod and thin rising vapors I judge; and here I will begin to mine.

Brute Neighbors

21   One day when I went out to my woodpile, or rather my pile of stumps, I observed two large ants, the one red, the other much larger, nearly half an inch long, and black, fiercely contending with one another. Having once got hold they never let go, but struggled and wrestled and rolled on the chips inces-santly. Looking farther, I was surprised to find that the chips were covered with such combatants, that it was not a *duellum,* but a *bellum,* a war between two races of ants, the red always pitted against the black, and frequently two red ones to one black. The legions of these Myrmidons covered all the hills and vales in my wood yard, and the ground was already strewn with the dead and dying, both red and black. It was the only battle which I have ever witnessed, the only battlefield I ever trod while the battle was raging; internecine war; the red republi-cans on the one hand, and the black imperial-ists on the other.

My greatest powers are centered there. My instinct tells me that my head is a tool for digging in the same way as some creatures use their snout and forepaws. I want to use my head to explore and understand these hills. I think that the richest discovery is somewhere around here. My divining rod[4] and the rising mists tell me it's nearby, so here is where I will begin to dig.

Brute Neighbors

21   One day when I went out to my woodpile I saw two large ants fighting fiercely with each other. One was red, and the other, which was much larger (nearly half an inch long) was black. Once they got hold of each other, they never let go but struggled and wrestled and rolled on the wood chips without letup. Looking more closely, I was surprised to find that the wood chips were covered with such fighters. It was not a duel but a battle, a war between two races of ants. The red were pitted against the black, and frequently there were two red to one black. Large numbers of these Myrmidons[5] covered all the hills and valleys in my wood yard. The ground was already covered with the dead and the dying, both red and black. It was the only battle that I have ever witnessed and the only battlefield I have ever walked upon while the battle was still raging. It was a war that was deadly to both sides—the red citizens' army on the one side and the black empire builders on the other.

---

4 **divining rod:** forked stick or branch that is supposed to indicate the presence of underground water when held over a source

5 **Myrmidons:** legendary people who took part with Achilles in the Trojan War

22   On every side they were engaged in deadly combat, yet without any noise that I could hear, and human soldiers never fought so resolutely. I watched a couple that were fast locked in each other's embraces, in a little sunny valley amid the chips, now at noonday prepared to fight till the sun went down, or life went out. The smaller red champion had fastened himself like a vice to his adversary's front, and through all the tumblings on that field never for an instant ceased to gnaw at one of his feelers near the root, having already caused the other to go by the board; while the stronger black one dashed him from side to side, and, as I saw on looking nearer, had already divested him of several of his members. They fought with more pertinacity than bulldogs. Neither manifested the least disposition to retreat. It was evident that their battle cry was conquer or die.

23   In the meanwhile there came along a single red ant on the hillside of this valley, evidently full of excitement, who either had despatched his foe, or had not yet taken part in the battle; probably the latter, for he had lost none of his limbs; whose mother had charged him to return with his shield or upon it. Or perchance he was some Achilles, who had nourished his wrath apart, and had now come to avenge or rescue his Patroclus.

24   He saw this unequal combat from afar—for the blacks were nearly twice the side of the red—he drew near with rapid pace till he stood on his guard within half an inch of the combatants; then, watching his opportunity, he sprang upon the black warrior, and commenced his operations near the root of his right

22   On every side they were involved in a deadly fight, yet without any noise that I could hear. Human soldiers never fought with more determination. I watched a pair of ants that were locked in each other's embrace in a little sunny valley in the middle of the wood chips. Though it was noon, they seemed prepared to fight until sunset or to the death. The smaller red defender had fastened himself like a vise to his enemy's front. Through all the rolling around on that field he never for a minute stopped chewing at one of his enemy's feelers near the root, having already chewed off the other feeler. Meanwhile, the stronger black ant flung the red one from side to side. On closer look, I saw that the black ant had already torn off several of the red ant's legs. They fought with more determination than bulldogs do. Neither showed any sign of wanting to retreat. It was obvious that their battle cry was "Conquer or die!"

23   Meanwhile, a single red ant, full of excitement, came on the hillside of this valley. He had either killed his foe, or had not yet taken part in the battle. Probably the latter was the case, for he had not yet lost any of his limbs. Perhaps his mother had commanded him to either return as a conqueror or to die trying. Or maybe he was some Achilles, who had been nursing his anger far away from the battlefield and had now come to seek revenge for his Patroclus or to rescue him.[6]

24   He saw this unequal battle from far off—for the blacks were nearly twice the size of the red—and he came close quickly until he stood on his guard within half an inch of the fighters. Watching for his opportunity, he sprang upon the black warrior and went to

---

6 **Achilles . . . Patroclus:** In the Greek legend of the *Iliad*, Achilles returned to the battlefield to pay back the enemy for the death of his friend, Patroclus.

foreleg, leaving the foe to select among his own members; and so there were three united for life, as if a new kind of attraction had been invented which put all other locks and cements to shame.

25   I should not have wondered by this time to find that they had their respective musical bands stationed on some eminent chip, and playing their national airs the while, to excite the slow and cheer the dying combatants. I was myself excited somewhat even as if they had been men. The more you think of it, the less the difference. And certainly there is not the fight recorded in Concord history, at least, if in the history of America, that will bear a moment's comparison with this, whether for the numbers engaged in it, or for the patriotism and heroism displayed. For numbers and for carnage it was an Austerlitz or Dresden. Concord Fight! Two killed on the patriots' side, and Luther Blanchard wounded! Why here every ant was a Buttrick—"Fire! for God's sake fire!"—and thousands shared the fate of Davis and Hosmer.

26   There was not one hireling there. I have no doubt that it was a principle they fought for, as much as our ancestors, and not to avoid a three-penny tax on their tea; and the results of this battle will be as important and memorable to those whom it concerns as those of the battle of Bunker Hill, at least.

work chewing the root of the black ant's right foreleg. This left his foe able to choose from among the red ant's limbs. The three ants were united for life. It was as if a new kind of glue had been invented that put all other locks and cements to shame.

25   It wouldn't have surprised me to see a musical band from each side playing its national anthems on a nearby wood chip in order to pump up the slower soldiers and cheer up the dying ones. I myself was almost as excited as if they had been men. The more you think of it, the less difference there is. And certainly there has never been a recorded battle in Concord history, or maybe in the history of the country, that could compare with this one in terms of numbers involved or patriotism and heroism displayed. For numbers and for bloodshed it was an Austerlitz or a Dresden.[7] Old newspapers reported, "The Battle of Concord! Two killed on the patriots' side, and Luther Blanchard wounded!" Why here, every ant was a Buttrick—"Fire! For God's sake fire!"—and thousands shared the fate of Davis and Hosmer.[8]

26   There was not one hired soldier here. I have no doubt that the ants were fighting over some principle, much as our ancestors did, and not over some three-penny tax on their tea either. The results of this battle will be as important and remembered to those whom it concerns as those at the Battle of Bunker Hill, at least.

7 **Austerlitz or a Dresden:** two cities in Czechoslovakia and Germany where Napoleon won major victories

8 **Luther Blanchard . . . Buttrick . . . Davis and Hosmer:** These are all soldiers in the Battle of Concord in 1775, the first battle in the Revolutionary War. Major John Buttrick was one of the leaders. Blanchard was wounded, and Davis and Hosmer were killed in that battle.

27   I took up the chip on which the three I have particularly described were struggling, carried it into my house, and placed it under a tumbler on my windowsill, in order to see the issue. Holding a microscope to the first-mentioned red ant, I saw that, though he was assiduously gnawing at the near foreleg of his enemy, having severed his remaining feeler, his own breast was all torn away, exposing what vitals he had there to the jaws of the black warrior, whose breastplate was apparently too thick for him to pierce; and the dark carbuncles of the sufferer's eyes shone with ferocity such as war only could excite.

28   They struggled half an hour longer under the tumbler, and when I looked again the black soldier had severed the heads of his foes from their bodies and the still living heads were hanging on either side of him like ghastly trophies at his saddlebow, still apparently as firmly fastened as ever, and he was endeavoring with feeble struggles, being without feelers and with only the remnant of a leg, and I know not how many other wounds, to divest himself of them; which at length, after half a hour more, he accomplished. I raised the glass, and he went off over the windowsill in that crippled state. Whether he finally survived that combat, and spent the remainder of his days in some Hôtel des Invalides, I do not know; but I thought that his industry would not be worth much thereafter.

29   I never learned which party was victorious, nor the cause of the war; but I felt for the rest of that day as if I had had my feelings excited and harrowed by witnessing the struggle, the ferocity and carnage, of a human battle before my door.

27   I picked up the wood chip on which the three that I have described were struggling, carried it into my house, and placed it under a glass on my windowsill, in order to see the outcome. Holding a microscope to the first-mentioned red ant, I saw that though he was busily chewing at the foreleg of his enemy, having severed the black ant's remaining feeler, the red ant's own breast was torn away. This exposed his insides to the jaws of the black warrior, whose breastplate was apparently too thick to be pierced. The coal black eyes of the suffering ant shone with a savage look that only happens in war.

28   The three of them struggled half an hour longer under the glass, and when I looked again, the black soldier had cut off the heads of his foes from their bodies. The still-living heads were hanging on either side of him like horrible trophies at his saddlebows. They were still, apparently, as firmly fastened to the black ant as ever. He was trying feebly—for he himself was without feelers, with only a portion of a leg, and I don't know how many other wounds—to rid himself of them. Finally, after half an hour more, he did. I raised the glass, and he went off over the windowsill in that crippled state. Whether he finally survived that battle and spent the remainder of his days in some hospital for invalids, I don't know. I didn't think he would be able to work much after that day.

29   I never learned which side was victorious, nor the cause of that war. However, for the rest of that day I felt as worked up and tormented by my witness of the fierce, bloody struggle as if I had witnessed a human battle before my door.

A Psalm of Life

Henry Wadsworth Longfellow

1   What the Heart of the Young Man
     Said to the Psalmist

2   Tell me not, in mournful numbers,
     Life is but an empty dream!—
     For the soul is dead that slumbers,
     And things are not what they seem.

3   Life is real! Life is earnest!
     And the grave is not its goal;
     Dust thou are, to dust returnest,
     Was not spoken of the soul.

4   Not enjoyment, and not sorrow,
     Is our destined end or way;
     But to act, that each tomorrow
     Find us farther than today.

5   Art is long, and Time is fleeting,
     And our hearts, through stout and brave,
     Still, like muffled drums, are beating
     Funeral marches to the grave.

6   In the world's broad field of battle,
     In the bivouac of Life,
     Be not like dumb, driven cattle!
     Be a hero in the strife!

A Psalm of Life

Henry Wadsworth Longfellow

1   What the young man's heart
    Said to the Psalmist[1]

2   I don't want to hear sad poems
    That say life is an empty dream!
    For the soul that sleeps is already dead,
    And things are not what they seem.

3   Life is real! Life is important!
    And the grave is not life's goal.
    You are dust. You return to dust,
    But that is not true of your soul.

4   Neither happiness nor sorrow
    Are our destiny or way,
    We must act, so each tomorrow
    Finds us farther than today.

5   Though poems are ageless, time flies,
    And our hearts though strong and brave,
    Still, like muffled drums are beating
    Funeral marches to the grave.

6   In the world's broad battlefield,
    As we journey through this life,
    Don't be like poor stupid cattle!
    Be a hero in the strife!

1 **Psalmist:** either David or Solomon, the writer of the Biblical
Psalms

7   Trust no Future, howe'er pleasant!
Let the dead Past bury its dead!
Act,—act in the living Present!
Heart within, and God o'erhead!

8   Lives of great men all remind us
WE can make our lives sublime,
And, departing, leave behind us
Footprints on the sands of time;

9   Footprints, that perhaps another,
Sailing o'er life's solemn main,
A forlorn and shipwrecked brother,
Seeing, shall take heart again.

10   Let us, then, be up and doing,
With a heart for any fate;
Still achieving, still pursuing,
Learn to labor and to wait.

7   Don't believe in a sweet future,
    Let the past stay buried and dead.
    Act now—in this present moment!
    Heart within and God overhead.

8   The lives of great men remind us,
    We can make our lives worthwhile.
    When we die we leave behind us
    Footprints on the sands of time.

9   Perhaps some day those footprints
    Will be found by a desperate brother,
    Whose ship was wrecked in the storms of life
    And needs new strength to go farther.

10 Rise up then and start doing,
    With a heart for any fate.
    Keep achieving! Keep on fighting!
    Learn to work hard and to wait.

Old Ironsides

Oliver Wendell Holmes

1   Ay, tear her tattered ensign down!
Long has it waved on high,
And many an eye has danced to see
That banner in the sky;
Beneath it rung the battle shout,
And burst the cannon's roar—
The meteor of the ocean air
Shall sweep the clouds no more.

2   Her deck, once red with heroes' blood,
Where knelt the vanquished foe,
When winds were hurrying o'er the flood,
And waves were white below,
No more shall feel the victor's tread,
Or now the conquered knee—
The harpies of the shore shall pluck
The eagle of the sea!

3   Oh, better that her shattered hulk
Should sink beneath the wave;
Her thunders shook the mighty deep,
And there should be her grave;
Nail to the mast her holy flag,
Set every threadbare sail,
And give her to the god of
    storms,
The lightning and the gale!

Old Ironsides

Oliver Wendell Holmes

1   Yes! tear her ragged flag down!
It waved so long on high.
Once, people felt great joy to see
That flag up in the sky.
Below, the shouts of battle rang,
Her cannons burst and roared,
The dazzling sight of the ocean skies
Will touch the clouds no more.

2   Her deck was red with heroes' blood.
There knelt defeated foes,
When winds blew over the water,
And the waves were white below.
She won't feel the step of the winners,
Nor feel the defeated man's knee.
She'll be robbed and looted and plundered—
This "eagle" of the sea.

3   This old, battered ship would be better off
If sunk beneath the waves.
Her sounds once shook the ocean floor
and there should be her grave.
Nail to the mast her holy flag,
Set every ragged sail,
And send her out to the open sea,
to meet lightning and the gale.

Stanzas on Freedom

James Russell Lowell

1   Men! whose boast it is that ye
Come of fathers brave and free,
If there breathe on earth a slave,
Are ye truly free and brave?
If ye do not feel the chain,
When it works a brother's pain,
Are ye not base slaves indeed,
Slaves unworthy to be freed?

2   Women! who shall one day bear
Sons to breathe New England air,
If ye hear, without a blush,
Deed to make the roused blood rush
Like red lava through your veins,
For your sisters now in chains—
Answer! are ye fit to be
Mother of the brave and free?

3   Is true Freedom but to break
Fetters for our own dear sake,
And, with leathern hearts, forget
That we owe mankind a debt?
No! true freedom is to share
All the chains our brothers wear,
And, with heart and hand, to be
Earnest to make others free!

Stanzas on Freedom

James Russell Lowell

1   Men who like to boast that they
    come from fathers brave and free—
    if on this earth there breathes a slave
    are you really free and brave?
    If you do not feel the chain
    when it brings a brother pain,
    aren't you a worthless slave indeed
    who does not deserve to be freed?

2   Women who will one day bear
    sons to breathe New England air—
    if you hear, without a blush,
    deeds that make your hot blood rush
    like red lava through your veins
    for your sisters now in chains—
    Answer! Do you deserve to be
    mothers of the brave and free?

3   Does true freedom only break
    chains for our own dear sake,
    and, with hard hearts, forget
    that we owe mankind a debt?
    No! True freedom means to share
    all the chains our brothers wear
    and with heart and hand, to be
    eager to make others free!

4   They are slaves who fear to speak
For the fallen and the weak;
They are slaves who will not choose
Hatred, scoffing, and abuse,
Rather than in silence shrink
From the truth they needs must think;
They are slaves who dare not be
In the right with two or three.

4   Slaves are those who fear to speak
for the fallen and the weak.
Slaves are those who will not choose
hatred, mocking, and abuse,
but instead in silence shrink
from the truth they dare not think.
Slaves are those afraid to be
In the right with two or three.

The Slaves by Jose Clemente Orozco

from Snowbound

John Greenleaf Whittier

A Winter Idyll

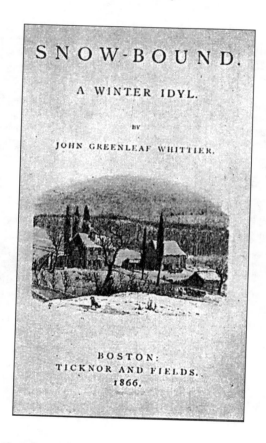

1   The sun that brief December day
Rose cheerless over hills of gray,
And, darkly circled, gave at noon

from Snowbound

John Greenleaf Whittier

A Winter Idyll

*Have you ever experienced a blizzard that closed
schools and stores and roads for several days?
"Snowbound" was written in the mid-1800s by New
England poet John Greenleaf Whittier. At that time in
our history most people lived in the country, close to
nature. Many were intimately familiar with the hills
and valleys, woods and streams in their immediate
vicinity. When a fierce winter storm struck, they had
no choice but to hunker down, keep the home fires
burning, and observe the transformation of their
world into a snow-covered wonder. Yet even in this
time there were chores to be done. Wood must be
brought in, or the people would freeze. The farm animals must be tended, or they would starve.*

*Some of the images in this poem may not be famil-
iar to you. Even so, if you slow down and try to
imagine a snowbound world without snowplows,
telephones, televisions, or radios, a world where every
household is cut off from every other household, you
will begin to understand what this poem is saying
today as well as when it was originally written.*

1   On that short December day
       the sun rose drearily over hills of gray.
    Dark circles surrounded the sun by noon,

A sadder light than waning moon.
Slow tracing down the thickening sky
2 Its mute and ominous prophecy,
A portent seeming less than threat,
It sank from sight before it set.
A chill no coat, however stout,
Of homespun stuff could quite shut out,
3 A hard, dull bitterness of cold,
 that checked, mid-vein, the circling race
Of lifeblood in the sharpened face,
The coming of the snowstorm told.
The wind blew east; we heard the roar
4 Of Ocean on his wintry shore,
And felt the strong pulse throbbing there
Beat with low rhythm our inland air.

Meanwhile we did our nightly chores—
Brought in the wood from out-of-doors,
5 Littered the stalls, and from the mows
Racked down the herd's-grass for the cows:
Heard the horse whinnying for his corn;
And, sharply clashing horn on horn,
Impatient down the stanchion rows
6 The cattle shake their walnut bows;
While, peering from his early perch
Upon the scaffold's pole of birch,
The cock his crested helmet bent
And down his querulous challenge sent.
7 Unwarmed by any sunset light
The gray day darkened into night,
A night made hoary with the swarm
And whirl-dance of the blinding storm,
As zigzag, wavering to and fro,
8 Crossed and recrossed the wingèd snow:
And ere the early bedtime came
The white drift piled the window frame,
And through the glass the clothesline posts

the sun's light was sadder than a waning moon's.
As the day drew on, the sky grew thick.
2   We felt the signs and an eerie sense
     of something coming.
Before it could set, the sun sank,
     and a chill set in that no coat,
     no matter how thick or warm, shut out.
3   It was a bone-chilling, bitter cold,
     that stopped the blood in our veins
     and drained the color from our faces.
We knew that a snowstorm was on its way.
The east wind blew; we heard the roar
4   of the winter wind on the ocean's shore
     while inland from the sea we felt
     its strong and rhythmic pulse.

Meanwhile, we did our nightly chores
     brought in the wood from out-of-doors,
5   put litter in the animals' stalls,
     raked down grass for the cows,
     heard the horse whinny for his corn.
Then down the row of cattle stalls
     the cattle shook their walnut yokes
6   and clashed their horns impatiently,
     while the rooster cocked his crested head,
     looked from his perch, and by and by
     sent forth a shrill, complaining cry.

7   Without the warmth of afternoon light
     the gray day deepened into night,
     the night was white with swirling snow
     that whirled and twirled and blinded sight,
     zigzagging wildly to and fro.
8   The snow moved on "wings" and before
     it was even early bedtime
     the snow drifts piled up to the window frames.
Outside the window the clothesline posts

Looked in like tall and sheeted ghosts.
9   So all night long the storm roared on:
The morning broke without a sun;
In tiny spherule traced with lines
Of Nature's goemetric signs,
In starry flake, and pellicle,
10   All day the hoary meteor fell;
And, when the second morning shone,
We looked upon a world unknown,
On nothing we could call our own.
Around the glistening wonder bent
11   The blue walls of the firmament,
No cloud above, no earth below—
A universe of sky and snow!
The old familiar sights of ours
Took marvelous shapes; strange domes and towers
12   Rose up where sty or corncrib stood,
Or garden wall, or belt of wood;
A smooth white mound the brush pile showed,
A fenceless drift what once was road;
The bridle post an old man sat
13   With loose-flung coat and high cocked hat;
The wellcurb had a Chinese roof;
And even the long sweep, high aloof,
In its slant splendor, seemed to tell
Of Pisa's leaning miracle.

14   A prompt, decisive man, no breath
Our father wasted: "Boys, a path!"
Well pleased (for when did farmer boy
Count such a summons less than joy?)
Our buskins on our feet we drew;
15   With mittened hands, and caps drawn low,
To guard our necks and ears from snow,

looked in like tall, white-sheeted ghosts.

9   Throughout the night the storm raged on,
    the morning came without a sun.
All day the white snow fell to earth
    in tiny spheres crisscrossed with lines,
    nature's geometric designs,
10   on snowflakes and on leaves.
And when the second morning came,
    we looked upon a world so strange—
    everything had changed.
Around the glistening, white-topped world
11   were wrapped the blue walls of the sky.
No cloud above, no earth below—
    a universe of sky and snow!
Old things that we once knew
    took on new shapes.
12 Pigpens, corncribs, walls, and trees
    were arches, towers—whatever you please.
The brush pile was a smooth white mound,
    no fences or roads could be found.
The bridle post became an old man who sat
13   with a flowing coat and a jaunty hat.
The wellcurb had a Chinese roof,
    and in the distance the long sweep,[1] for some reason,
    slanting and covered in splendid snow,
    looked like a small Leaning Tower of Pisa.

14 Our father, who always knew what to do,
    wasted no words, said, "Boys, a path!"
How pleased we were, for what farm boy
    would not be happy with such a chore?
Quickly we laced up our boots,
15   put on mittens, pulled our caps low
    to protect our necks and ears from snow.

---

1 **sweep:** long pole, with a bucket at one end, that is used to get water from a well

We cut the solid whiteness through.
And, where the drift was deepest, made
A tunnel walled and overlaid
With dazzling crystal: we had read
Of rare Aladdin's wondrous cave,
And to our own his name we gave,
With many a wish the luck were ours
To test his lamp's supernal powers.
We reached the barn with merry din,
And roused the prisoned brutes within.
The old horse thrust his long head out,
and grave with wonder gazed about;
The cock his lusty greeting said,
And forth his speckled harem led;
The oxen lashed their tails, and hooked,
And mild reproach of hunger looked;
The hornèd patriarch of the sheep,
Like Egypt's Amun roused from sleep,
Shook his sage head with gesture mute,
And emphasized with stamp of foot.

All day the gusty north wind bore
The loosening drift its breath before;
Low circling round its southern zone,
The sun through dazzling snow-mist shone.
No church bell lent its Christian tone
To the savage air, no social smoke
Curled over woods of snow-hung oak.
A solitude made more intense
By dreary-voicèd elements,
The shrieking of the mindless wind,
The moaning tree boughs swaying blind,
And on the glass the unmeaning beat
Of ghostly fingertips of sleet.
Beyond the circle of our hearth
No welcome sound of toil or mirth

16

17

18

19

20

21

22

We cut through the solid white,
    Through the deepest part a tunnel was made
      with walls and roof of dazzling "crystal."
16   We had read of Aladdin's wonderful cave
      and decided to name our cave after his.
How we wished we had Aladdin's luck
    and could do all he did with his magical lamp.

17   In high spirits we reached the barn,
      woke up the beasts who were prisoners there.
The old horse stuck his long head out,
    Thoughtfully, he looked about.
The rooster welcomed us and then
18   led forth his speckled band of hens.
Switching their tails and pretending to charge
    the oxen scolded us for coming so late.
The sheepbuck, granddaddy of all the sheep,
    like Egypt's Amun[2] woken from sleep,
19   shook his old head and without a sound
    made his point with a stomp on the ground.

The blustering north wind blew all day,
    and with its breath it loosened the drifts.
Circling low in its southern zone,
20   the sun through the dazzling snow-mist shone.
No church bell gave a Christian tone
    to the savage air. No smoke rose
    over woods of oaks hung low with snow.
Our isolation became more intense
21   by the dreary voices of the elements—
    the shrieking sound of the endless wind,
    the moaning, swaying as the tree boughs bent,
    and on our windowpanes there beat
    the ghostly fingertips of sleet.
22   Beyond our fireplace and home
    there was no sound—we were all alone.

2 **Amun:** Egyptian god often represented with a ram's head

Unbound the spell, and testified
Of human life and thought outside.
We minded that the sharpest ear
23   The buried brooklet could not hear,
The music of whose liquid lip
Had been to us companionship,
And, in our lonely life, had grown
To have an almost human tone.

24   As night drew on, and, from the crest
Of wooded knolls that ridged the west,
The sun, a snow-blown traveler, sank
From sight beneath the smothering bank,
We piled, with care, our nightly stack
25   Of wood against the chimney back—
The oaken log, green, huge, and thick,
And on its top the stout backstick;
The knotty forestick laid apart,
And filled between with curious art
26   The ragged brush; then, hovering near,
We watched the first red blaze appear,
Heard the sharp crackle, caught the gleam
On whitewashed wall and sagging beam,
Until the old, rude-finished room
27   Burst, flowerlike, into rosy bloom;
While radiant with a mimic flame
Outside the sparkling drift became,
And through the bare-boughed lilac tree
Our own warm hearth seemed blazing free.
28   The crane and pendent trammels showed,
The Turks' heads on the andirons glowed;
While childish fancy, prompt to tell
The meaning of the miracle,
Whispered the old rhyme: *"Under the tree,*
29   *When fire outdoors burns merrily,*
There the witches are making tea."

Nothing broke the spell or showed
    a sign of human life at all.
No one in our house could hear
23   the little brook buried under the snow.
That brook whose liquid sounds had been
    our ever-present and welcome friend.
In our lonely life the brook had grown
    to almost sound like a human voice.

24   It was night again, and from the top
    of the small wooded hills that lined the west,
    the sun, like a traveler blown over by snow,
    sank from sight beneath a drift.
We carefully piled our nightly stack
25   of wood against the chimney's back—
    an oak log, huge and thick and green
    and on its top the tough backstick.
At the front of the hearth was a knotty log
    and between these logs with an arty flair
26   brushwood was piled; then waiting there
    we watched the first red flame appear,
    heard the sharp crackle, saw it gleam
    on the whitewashed wall and the sagging beams.
Simply furnished, the rough old room
27   burst, like a flower, into bloom.
Outside, you could see the reflection of flame
    on the sparkling snowdrift, as it came
    through the bare boughs of the lilac tree
    where our warm fire was blazing free.
28   The iron hooks in the fireplace shone,
The Turkish heads on the andirons[3] glowed.
We whispered an old rhyme as we watched the light
    and tried to explain the fantastic sights:
    "Under the tree,
29   *when an outdoor fire burns merrily*
    that's where the witches are making tea."

3 **Turkish heads . . . andirons:** Andirons are the metal supports
that hold firewood in a fireplace. Whittier calls the rounded tops
of the andirons "Turks' heads" because Turkish men wore turbans,
and the tops of the andirons reminded Whittier of turbans.

The moon above the eastern wood
Shone at its full; the hill range stood
Transfigured in the silver flood,
30   Its blown snows flashing cold and keen,
Dead white, save where some sharp ravine
Took shadow, or the somber green
Of hemlocks turned to pitchy black
Against the whiteness at their back.

31   For such a world and such a night
Most fitting that unwarming light,
Which only seemed where'er it fell
To make the coldness visible.

Shut in from all the world without,
32   We sat the clean-winged hearth about,
Content to let the north wind roar
In baffled rage at pane and door,
While the red logs before us beat
The frost line back with tropic heat;
33   And ever, when a louder blast
Shook beam and rafter as it passed,
The merrier up its roaring draft
The great throat of the chimney laughed;
The house dog on his paws outspread

34   Laid to the fire his drowsy head,
The cat's dark silhouette on the wall
A couchant tiger's seemed to fall;
And, for the winter fireside meet,
Between the andirons' straddling feet,
35   The mug of cider simmered
     slow,
The apples sputtered in a row,
And, close at hand, the basket
     stood
With nuts from brown October's
     wood.

Above the east woods a full moon shone
    which on that night
    looked glorious in the silver light.
30 The blowing snows were cold and sharp,
    the hills completely capped with snow
    except in some deep hollows below
    where shadows fell, and the dark green
    hemlocks looked almost black
    compared to the whiteness at their back.
31 And on this world and on this night
    there fell a cold that was oddly right
    and everywhere the moonlight beamed
    the coldness was more clearly seen.

    Shut in from the outside world,
32   we sat around the clean-swept hearth,
    content to let the north wind roar
    and beat against windowpanes and doors,
    while our blazing fire with its tropical heat
    protected us from the cold and sleet.
33 Whenever the wind with a loud blast
    shook the house roughly as it passed,
    our chimney laughed
    and sent up its throat
    a cheerful, roaring hot-air draft.
    Our dog by the fireside made his bed,
34   stretched out his paws, laid down his head.
    The cat's dark silhouette on the wall
    looked like a tiger awake and on call.
    Between the andirons' "feet" in the hearth

35   a mug of cider simmered slow.
    Apples were cooking in a row.
    And nearby a basket stood
    with nuts from brown October woods.

from Narrative in the Life of Frederick Douglass

Frederick Douglass

1   I left Master Thomas's house, and went to live with Mr. Covey, on the 1ˢᵗ of January, 1833. I was now, for the first time in my life, a field hand. In my new employment, I found myself even more awkward than a country boy appeared to be in a large city. I had been at my new home but one week before Mr. Covey gave me a very severe whipping, cutting my back, causing the blood to run, and raising ridges on my flesh as large as my little finger. The details of this affair are as follows: Mr. Covey

2   sent me, very early in the morning of one of our coldest days in the month of January, to the woods, to get a load of wood. He gave me a team of unbroken oxen. He told me which was the in-hand ox, and which the off-hand one. He then tied the end of a large rope around the horns of the in-hand ox, and gave me the other end of it, and told me, if the oxen started to run, that I must hold on upon the rope. I had never driven oxen before, and of course I was very awkward. I, however, succeeded in getting to the edge of the woods with little difficulty; but I had got a very

3   few rods into the woods, when the oxen took fright, and started full tilt, carrying the cart against trees,

from Narrative in the Life of Frederick Douglass

Frederick Douglass

1   On January 1, 1833, I left Master Thomas's house and went to live with Mr. Covey. For the first time in my life I was a farm hand. In my new work I felt as out of place as a country boy in a big city. I had been at my new home only one week before Mr. Covey gave me a terrible beating that bloodied my back with welts as big as my little finger. This is what happened.

2   Early one morning, on one of the coldest days in January, Mr. Covey sent me to get a load of wood from the woods. He gave me a team of unbroken oxen and told me which was the in-hand ox and which was the off-hand one. Then he tied the end of a big rope around the horns of the in-hand ox and gave the other end to me. He told me that if the oxen started to run, I should hold on. I had never driven oxen before and, of course, was very awkward at it. However, I managed to get to the edge of the woods without much trouble.

3   When I got into the woods 50–60 feet, the oxen got frightened and started running at full speed.

and over stumps, in the most frightful manner. I expected every moment that my brains would be dashed out against the trees. After running thus for a considerable distance, they finally upset the cart, dashing it with great force against a tree, and threw themselves into a dense thicket. How I escaped death, I do not know. There I was, entirely alone, in a thick wood, in a place new to me. My cart was upset and shattered, my oxen were entangled among the young trees, and there was none to help me. After a long spell of effort, I succeeded in getting my cart righted, my oxen disentangled, and again yoked to the cart. I now proceeded with my team to the place where I had, the day before, been chopping wood, and loaded my cart pretty heavily, thinking in this way to tame my oxen. I then proceeded on my way home. I

4   had now consumed one-half of the day. I got out of the woods safely, and now felt out of danger. I stopped my oxen to open the woods gate; and just as I did so, before I could get hold of my ox rope, the oxen again started, rushed through the gate, catching it between the wheel and the body of the cart, tearing it to pieces, and coming within a few inches of crushing me against the gatepost. Thus twice, in one short day, I escaped death by the merest chance. On my return,

5   I told Mr. Covey what had happened, and how it happened. He ordered me to return to the woods again immediately. I did so, and he followed on after me. Just as I got into the woods, he came up and told me to stop my cart, and that he would teach me how to trifle away my time, and break gates. He then went to a large gum tree, and with his axe cut three large switches, and, after trimming them up neatly with his pocketknife, he ordered me to take off my clothes. I made him no answer, but stood with my clothes on.

They rammed the cart against trees and over stumps. It was frightful! I thought every moment that my brains would be dashed against the trees. After running quite a ways, they finally upset the cart, smashed it against a tree, and threw themselves into the dense underbrush of the woods. I don't know how I made it out alive. There I was, all alone in the middle of an unfamiliar woods. My cart was turned over and broken, the oxen were tangled among the young trees, and there was no one to help me. After working for a long time, I managed to get my cart right side up and the oxen free and hitched to the cart. I went back to the place where I had been chopping wood the day before and loaded the cart heavily, thinking this was the way to tame the oxen. Then I set out for home.

4   By now I had used up half of the day. I got out of the woods safely and thought I was out of danger. When I got to the gate, however, I stopped the oxen to open it, and in that brief moment before I got hold of my rope again, the oxen charged through the gate. The gate got caught between the wheel and the body, and was torn to pieces. I was almost crushed against the gatepost. So twice in one short day I was almost killed.

5   When I got back I told Mr. Covey what had happened and how. He ordered me back to the woods immediately. I went and he followed. Just as I got to the woods, he came up and told me to stop the cart. He said he would teach me how to waste time and break gates. He went to a large gum tree and with his ax cut three large switches. After trimming them neatly with his pocket knife, he ordered me to take off my clothes. I didn't answer him but did not take off my clothes either. He repeated his order, but

He repeated his order. I still made him no answer, nor did I move to strip myself. Upon this he rushed at me with the fierceness of a tiger, tore off my clothes, and lashed me till he had worn out his switches, cutting me so savagely as to leave the marks visible for a long time after. This whipping was the first of a number just like it, and for similar offenses.

6   I lived with Mr. Covey one year. During the first six months of that year, scarce a week passed without his whipping me. I was seldom free from a sore back. My awkwardness was almost always his excuse for whipping me. We were worked fully up to the point of endurance. Long before day we were up, our horses fed, and by the first approach of day we were off to the field with our hoes and ploughing teams. Mr. Covey gave us enough to eat, but scarce time to eat it. We were often less than five minutes taking our meals. We were often in the field from the first approach of day till its last lingering ray had left us; and at saving-fodder time, midnight often caught us in the field binding blades.

7   Covey would be out with us. The way he used to stand it, was this. He would spend the most of his afternoons in bed. He would then come out fresh in the evening, ready to urge us on with his words, example, and frequently with the whip. Mr. Covey was one of the few slaveholders who could and did work with his hands. He was a hardworking man. He knew by himself just what a man or a boy could do. There was no deceiving him. His work went on in his

8   absence almost as well as in his presence; and he had the faculty of making us feel that he was ever present with us. This he did by surprising us. He seldom

I still did not answer him, nor did I start to undress. He came after me like a wild tiger, tore off my clothes, and beat me until he had worn out his switches. I was so badly cut up that I had marks on my body for a long time afterwards. That was the first whipping of many that I got for doing something like that.

6   I lived with Mr. Covey a year. During the first six months hardly a week passed without him whipping me. I almost always had a sore, raw back, and my clumsiness was almost always his excuse for the whipping. He worked us as hard as possible. Long before daylight we were up and had our horses fed. As soon as dawn arrived, we were out in the field with our hoes and plowing teams. Mr. Covey gave us enough to eat but hardly any time to eat it; we often had less than five minutes to eat our meals. We were often in the field from dawn till dark and at haying time, until midnight when we were in the field tying bundles.

7   Covey was often out in the field with us, but he spent most of the afternoon in bed. In the evening he'd come out rested and ready to work alongside us. Through his words and with his whip he kept us working. Mr. Covey was one of the few slave masters who could and did work with his hands, and I'll admit he was a hardworking man himself. Furthermore, he knew exactly what a man or a boy could accomplish. which meant there was no tricking him.

8   We worked almost as well when he was absent as when he was present because he had a way of making us feel as though he was always with us. He did

approached the spot where we were at work openly, if he could do it secretly. He always aimed at taking us by surprise. Such was his cunning, that we used to call him, among ourselves, "the snake." When we were at work in the cornfield, he would sometimes crawl on his hands and knees to avoid detection, and all at once he would rise nearly in our midst, and scream out, "Ha, ha! Come, come! Dash on, dash on!" This being his mode of attack, it was never safe to stop a single minute. His comings were like a thief in the night. He appeared to us as being ever at hand. He was under every tree, behind every stump, in every bush, and at every window, on the plantation. He would sometimes mount his horse, as if bound to St. Michael's, a distance of seven miles, and in half an hour afterwards you would see him coiled up in the corner of the wood fence, watching every motion of the slaves. He would, for this purpose, leave his horse tied up in the woods. Again, he would some-times walk up to us, and give us orders as though he was upon the point of starting on a long journey, turn his back upon us, and make as though he was going to the house to get ready; and, before he would get halfway thither, he would turn short and crawl into a fence corner, or behind some tree, and there watch us till the going down of the sun. . . .

9   If at any one time of my life more than another, I was made to drink the bitterest dregs of slavery, that time was during the first six months of my stay with Mr. Covey. We were worked in all weathers. It was never too hot or too cold; it could never rain, blow, hail, or snow, too hard for us to work in the field. Work, work, work, was scarcely more the order of the day than of the night. The longest days were too short for him, and the shortest nights too long for him. I was somewhat unmanageable when I first

this by catching us off guard. He rarely came upon us in the open if he could sneak up on us. He always tried to surprise us. He was so sneaky that among ourselves we called him "the snake." When we were at work in the cornfield, he would crawl through the rows on his hands and knees and then stand up suddenly and say, "Aha! All right now! Get to work!" Since this was the way he operated, you were never safe for a minute. He came like a thief in the night, and he seemed to be everywhere at once. He was under every tree, behind every stump, in every bush, and at every window on the plantation. He would sometimes jump on his horse as if he was going to St. Michael's, about seven miles away, and half an hour later you'd see him coiled up in the corner of the fence, watching every movement of the slaves. For this reason, he left his horse tied up in the woods. At other times he would walk up to us and give us orders as though he was about to leave on a long journey, turn his back on us and pretend that he was going to the house to get ready. Yet, before he got halfway to the house, he would turn and crawl into a corner of the fence, or behind a tree, and from there watch us until the end of the day. . . .

9 My first six months with Mr. Covey were the most miserable slavery experiences I had. He made us work in all kinds of weather. It was never too hot or too cold to work. It never rained, blew, hailed, or snowed too hard for us to work in the field. By day or by night it was work and more work. The longest days were too short for Mr. Covey, and the shortest nights were too long. I was somewhat hard to handle when I first arrived, but after six months of Mr. Covey's discipline, I was broken in body, soul, and

went there, but a few months of this discipline tamed me. Mr. Covey succeeded in breaking me. I was broken in body, soul, and spirit. My natural elasticity was crushed, my intellect languished, the disposition to read departed, the cheerful spark that lingered about my eye died; the dark night of slavery closed in upon me; and behold a man transformed into a brute!

10 Sunday was my only leisure time. I spent this in a sort of beastlike stupor, between sleep and wake, under some large tree. At times I would rise up, a flash of energetic freedom would dart through my soul, accompanied with a faint beam of hope, that flickered for a moment, and then vanished. I sank down again, mourning over my wretched condition. I was sometimes prompted to take my life, and that of Covey, but was prevented by a combination of hope and fear. My sufferings on this plantation seem now like a dream rather than a stern reality. . . .

11 I have already intimated that my condition was much worse, during the first six months of my stay at Mr. Covey's, than in the last six. The circumstances leading to the change in Mr. Covey's course toward me form an epoch in my humble history. You have seen how a man was made a slave; you shall see how a slave was made a man. On one of the hottest days of the month of August, 1833, Bill Smith, William Hughes, a slave named Eli, and myself, were engaged in fanning wheat. Hughes was clearing the fanned wheat from before the fan. Eli was turning, Smith was feeding, and I was carrying wheat to the fan. The work was simple, requiring strength rather than intellect; yet, to one entirely unused to such work, it came very hard. About three
12 o' clock of that day, I broke down; my strength failed me; I was seized with a violent aching of the head,

spirit. My natural optimism was crushed, and my mind grew weak. I had, in fact, no interest in reading anything, and there was no spark of life in my eyes. Slavery's dark night closed in on me. At last I was changed from a man without any conscious thoughts or hopes.

10   Sunday was my only free time. I spent this time in a drugged state, half-awake, half-asleep, under a big tree. I would wake up, feeling a flash of energy through my soul and a faint glint of hope, which flickered and soon died. Then I would slump down again, moaning about the awful state I was in. I sometimes thought about taking my own life and that of Covey but did not act on that thought out of a combination of hope and fear. My suffering during that time seems now like a dream rather than something that really happened. . . .

11   I have already mentioned that my situation was much worse during the first six months with Mr. Covey than in the second. Something happened that changed my life. You have seen how a man became a slave. Now you will see how a slave became a man. On one of the hottest days in August of 1833, Bill Smith, William Hughes, a slave named Eli, and I were working at separating the wheat from the chaff. Hughes was clearing the fanned wheat in front of the fan. Eli was turning the fan, Smith was feeding the wheat, and I was carrying the wheat to the fan. The work was simple and took strength rather than brains, but to someone like me, who was not used to this kind of work, it was exhausting.

12   About three o'clock on that day, I broke down. My strength gave out, my head began to ache something

attended with extreme dizziness; I trembled in every limb. Finding what was coming, I nerved myself up, feeling it would never do to stop work. I stood as long as I could stagger to the hopper with grain. When I could stand no longer, I fell, and felt as if held down by an immense weight. The fan of course stopped; every one had his own work to do; and no one could do the work of the other, and have his own go on at the same time.

13   Mr. Covey was at the house, about one hundred yards from the treading-yard where we were fanning. On hearing the fan stop, he left immediately, and came to the spot where we were. He hastily inquired what the matter was. Bill answered that I was sick, and there was no one to bring wheat to the fan. I had by this time crawled away under the side of the post and rail fence by which the yard was enclosed, hoping to find relief by getting out of the sun. He then asked where I was. He was told by one of the hands. He came to the spot, and after looking at me awhile, asked me what was the matter. I told him as well as I could, for I scarce had strength to speak. He then gave me a savage kick in the side, and told me to get up. I tried to do so, but fell back in the attempt. He gave me another kick, and again told me to rise. I

14 again tried, and succeeded in gaining my feet; but, stooping to get the tub with which I was feeding the fan, I again staggered and fell. While down in this situation, Mr. Covey took up the hickory slat with which Hughes has been striking off the half-bushel measure, and with it gave me a heavy blow upon the head, making a large wound, and the blood ran freely; and with this again told me to get up. I made no effort to comply, having now made up my mind to let him do his worst. In a short time after receiving

awful, and I felt extremely dizzy. My legs and arms were shaking violently. When I realized what was happening, I tried to go on, knowing that I would not be allowed to stop working. I stood for as long as I could stagger to the hopper with the grain. Finally, I couldn't stand up any longer. I fell and felt like a mountain had landed on top of me. The fan, of course, stopped. Everyone had his own part of the work to do, and no one could do the other person's work and his own at the same time.

13   Mr. Covey was at the house, about a hundred yards from where we were working. When he heard the fan stop, he came over immediately and quickly asked what the problem was. Bill said that I was sick, and there was no one to bring the wheat to the fan. By this time I had crawled away under the fence, hoping to feel better once I was out of the sun. Covey asked where I was and was told by one of the men. He came to me and after looking at me for a while asked me what the matter was. I told him as well as I could, but I had barely enough strength to speak. He then gave me a vicious kick in the side and told me to get up. I tried to but fell back again. He gave me another kick and told me to get up.

14   This time I managed to get to my feet, but as I reached out to the tub for support, I fell again. While I was down, Mr. Covey picked up the hickory stick that Hughes had used to level off his measuring bucket and gave me a hard blow on the head. I now had a large wound with the blood running freely. Again, Covey told me to get up. I didn't even try to do so. I made up my mind to let him do whatever brutal thing he had in mind. In a little while my head felt a little better, but by this time Mr. Covey had left me alone.

this blow, my head grew better. Mr. Covey had now left me to my fate. At this moment I resolved, for the
15   first time, to go to my master, enter a complaint, and ask his protection. In order to do this, I must that afternoon walk seven miles; and this, under the circumstances, was truly a severe undertaking. I was exceedingly feeble; made so as much by the kicks and blows which I received, as by the severe fit of sickness to which I had been subjected. I, however, watched my chance, while Covey was looking in an opposite direction, and started for St. Michael's. I succeeded in getting a considerable distance on my way to the woods, when Covey discovered me, and called after me to come back, threatening what he would do if I did not come. I disregarded both his calls and his threats, and made my way to the woods as fast as my feeble state would allow; and thinking I
16   might be overhauled by him if I kept the road, I walked through the woods, keeping far enough from the road to avoid detection, and near enough to prevent losing my way. I had not gone far before my little strength again failed me. I could go no farther. I fell down, and lay for a considerable time. The blood was yet oozing from the wound on my head. For a time I thought I should bleed to death; and think now that I should have done so, but that the blood so matted my hair as to stop the wound. After lying
17   there about three-quarters of an hour, I nerved myself up again, and started on my way, through bogs and briers, barefooted and bareheaded, tearing my feet sometimes at nearly every step; and after a journey of about seven miles, occupying some five hours to perform it, I arrived at master's store. I then presented an appearance enough to affect any but a heart of iron. From the crown of my head to my feet, I was covered with blood. My hair was all clotted with dust and blood; my shirt was stiff with blood.

15   At that moment I decided to go to my original master, enter a complaint against Mr. Covey, and ask for protection. To do this, I would have to walk seven miles that afternoon. Given the state I was in, this was no easy matter. I was very weak, as much from the kicks and blows as from being sick, but I waited for my chance to move. While Covey was looking in the opposite direction, I took off for St. Michael's. I got quite a ways to the woods when Covey spied me and called me to come back. He threatened me with what he would do if I did not come back, but I paid no attention to his calls and threats and got to the woods as fast as my weak condition let me.

16   Thinking he might catch me if I stayed on the road, I walked through the woods, staying on the edge so that I could see where I was going but far enough in so that I could not be seen from the road. I hadn't gone very far before I collapsed. I lay in the woods for quite a while. Blood still oozed from the wound on my head, and for a while I thought I would bleed to death, but the blood matted my hair and helped stop the bleeding.

17   After about 45 minutes, I pulled myself together and started out again. Bareheaded and barefooted, I passed through swamps and thick undergrowth that cut my feet. It took me about five hours to go seven miles, but finally I arrived at master's store. I looked so pitiful that anyone who didn't have a heart of stone would have been moved. I was covered with blood from head to toe. My hair was dusty and bloody. My shirt was stiff with blood, and my legs and feet were cut in many places with briers and

My legs and feet were torn in sundry places with briers and thorns, and were also covered with blood. I suppose I looked like a man who had escaped a den of wild beasts, and barely escaped them. In this state I appeared before my master, humbly entreating him to interpose his authority for my protection. I told

18   him all the circumstances as well as I could, and it seemed, as I spoke, at times to affect him. He would then walk the floor, and seek to justify Covey by saying he expected I deserved it. He asked me what I wanted. I told him, to let me get a new home; that as sure as I lived with Mr. Covey again, I should live with but to die with him; that Covey would surely kill me; he was in a fair way for it. Master Thomas ridiculed the idea that there was any danger of Mr. Covey's killing me, and said that he knew Mr. Covey; that he was a good man, and that he could not think of taking me from him; that, should he do so, he would lose the whole year's wages; that I belonged to Mr. Covey for one year, and that I must go back to him, come what might; and that I must not trouble him with any more stories, or that he would himself *get hold of me*. After threatening me thus, he gave me a very large dose of salts, telling me that I might remain in St. Michael's that night (it being quite late), but that I must be off back to Mr. Covey's early in the morning; and that if I did not, he would *get hold of me*, which meant that he would whip me. I

19   remained all night, and, according to his orders, I started off to Covey's in the morning (Saturday morning), wearied in body and broken in spirit. I got no supper that night, or breakfast that morning. I reached Covey's about nine o' clock; and just as I was getting over the fence that divided Mrs. Kemp's fields from ours, out ran Covey with his cowskin, to give me another whipping. Before he could reach me, I succeeded in getting to the cornfield; and as the corn

thorns. I looked like someone who had escaped a pack of wild animals. In this pitiful state I found my master and humbly begged him to step in and to use his power to protect me.

18   As best I could, I told him everything that had happened, and he seemed, at times, to be sympathetic. But then he would pace the floor and try to justify Covey by saying that I probably deserved what I had gotten. He asked what I wanted, and I asked him to get me a new home. I told him that if I lived with Mr. Covey again, I would surely die. Covey would certainly kill me. Master Thomas laughed at me for saying that Mr. Covey might kill me. He said that he knew Mr. Covey, and that he was a good man. Master Thomas said that he could in no way interfere because if he did, he would lose the whole year's wages that he was being paid by Covey for my services. Thomas said I had to go back to Covey, no matter what, and that I should not bother my master with any more stories, or he himself would give me a beating. After threatening me, he gave me salts for my wounds and told me I could stay in St. Michael's that night. I must, however, be on my way back early the next day, and that if I didn't go, he would give me a whipping himself.

19   I stayed all night and started back to Covey's in the morning, a Saturday. I was exhausted in body and broken in spirit. I had had no supper the night before and no breakfast that morning and reached Covey's about nine o'clock. Just as I was climbing over the fence that divided Mrs. Kemp's fields from ours, Covey ran out with his cowskin to give me another whipping. Before he could reach me, I ran into the cornfield, which was high enough to hide me.

was very high, it afforded me the means of hiding. He seemed very angry, and searched for me a long time. My behavior was altogether unaccountable. He finally gave up the chase, thinking, I suppose, that I must come home for something to eat; he would give himself no further trouble in looking for me. I spent

20   that day mostly in the woods, having the alternative before me—to go home and be whipped to death, or stay in the woods and be starved to death. That night, I fell in with Sandy Jenkins, a slave with whom I was somewhat acquainted. Sandy had a free wife who lived about four miles from Mr. Covey's; and it being Saturday, he was on his way to see her. I told him my circumstances, and he very kindly invited me to go home with him. I went home with him, and talked this whole matter over, and got his advice as to what course it was best for me to pursue. I found

21   Sandy an old adviser. He told me, with great solemnity, I must go back to Covey; but that before I went, I must go with him into another part of the woods, where there was a certain *root*, which, if I would take some of it with me, carrying it *always on my right side*, would render it impossible for Mr. Covey, or any other white man, to whip me. He said he had carried it for years; and since he had done so, he had never received a blow, and never expected to while he carried it. I at first rejected the idea, that the simple carrying of a root in my pocket would have any such effect as he had said, and was not disposed to take it; but Sandy impressed the necessity with much earnestness, telling me it could do no harm, if it did no good. To please him, I at length took the root, and, according to his direction, carried it upon my right

22   side. This was Sunday morning. I immediately started for home; and upon entering the yard gate, out came Mr. Covey on his way to meeting. He spoke to me very kindly, bade me drive the pigs from a lot

Covey was very angry and searched for me a long time. I don't exactly know why I did what I did, but Covey finally gave up looking for me, probably thinking that I would have to come home to eat and he wouldn't bother with me until then.

20   I spent most of the day in the woods, thinking of the two choices before me—to go home and be whipped to death or to stay in the woods and starve to death. That night I met up with Sandy Jenkins, a slave that I knew slightly. Sandy had a free wife who lived about four miles from Mr. Covey's. Because it was Saturday, he was going to see her. I told him what had happened, and he kindly invited me to go home with him. I did so and talked over the whole matter with him and got his advice on the best thing to do.

21   Now Sandy believed in the old ways. He told me, very seriously, that I had to go back to Covey, but that before I did, I should go into the woods with him to get a certain root. He told me that if I carried this root on my right side, no white man, including Mr. Covey, would be able to whip me. He said that he had done so for years and had never had any trouble. At first I considered his idea worthless. How could carrying a simple root have such a powerful effect? But Sandy insisted that the root would help me and said that at the least it could do no harm, even if it didn't work for me. Finally, to please him, I took the root and carried it on my right side.

22   It was a Sunday morning when I started out for home, and as soon as I got in the gate I saw Mr. Covey on his way to church. He spoke very kindly to me and asked me to drive the pigs from a nearby lot.

near by, and passed on toward the church. Now, this singular conduct of Mr. Covey really made me begin to think that there was something in the *root* which Sandy had given me; and had it been on any other day than Sunday, I could have attributed the conduct to no other cause than the influence of that root; and as it was, I was half inclined to think the root to be something more than I at first had taken it to be. All went well till Monday morning. On this morning, the

23   virtue of the *root* was fully tested. Long before day-light, I was called to go and rub, curry, and feed, the horses. I obeyed, and was glad to obey. But whilst thus engaged, whilst in the act of throwing down some blades from the loft, Mr. Covey entered the sta-ble with a long rope; and just as I was half out of the loft, he caught hold of my legs, and was about tying me. As soon as I found what he was up to, I gave a sudden spring, and as I did so, he holding to my legs, I was brought sprawling on the stable floor. Mr.
24   Covey seemed now to think he had me, and could do what he pleased; but at this moment—from whence came the spirit I don't know—I resolved to fight; and, suiting my action to the resolution, I seized Covey hard by the throat; and as I did so, I rose. He held on to me, and I to him. My resistance was so entirely unexpected, that Covey seemed taken all aback. He trembled like a leaf. This gave me assurance, and I held him uneasy, causing the blood to run where I touched him with the ends of my fingers. Mr. Covey soon called out to Hughes for help. Hughes came, and, while Covey held me, attempted to tie my right hand. While he was in the act of doing so, I watched my chance, and gave him a heavy kick close under the ribs. This kick fairly sickened Hughes, so that he left me in the hands of Mr. Covey. This kick had the

Then he went on his way to church. This odd behavior on the part of Mr. Covey got me thinking that maybe the root which Sandy had given me really did have some power. If it had been any day except Sunday, I would have had no choice but to assume that it was definitely the root that had protected me. Even though it was Sunday, I was half-tempted to think the root was more powerful than I had at first thought it was. In fact, everything was fine until Monday morning. That's when the root was fully tested.

23   Well before sunrise I was called to go and rub, curry, and feed the horses. I obeyed, happy to do so. But while I was throwing down some hay from the loft, Mr. Covey came into the stable with a long rope. I was half out of the loft, and he started to grab my legs in order to tie me up. As soon as I realized what he was doing, I made a sudden, unexpected move. Because he was holding my legs, I fell to the stable floor.

24   Mr. Covey seemed to think he had me where he wanted me, but something rose up in me—I'm not sure how it happened—and I decided to fight him. I grabbed Covey by the throat and as I did so, I rose to my feet. He held onto me, and I held unto him. Covey was taken by surprise. He hadn't expected me to resist, and he now trembled like a leaf. This gave me confidence. I held him so hard that blood ran where my fingers gripped him. I wasn't sure what to do next, but then Mr. Covey called to Hughes for help. Hughes came and tried to tie my right hand as Covey held me. I waited for a chance and then gave Hughes a hard kick under the ribs. The kick made Hughes sick, and he left me in the hands of Covey. The kick seemed to have weakened Covey as well as Hughes. When he saw Hughes doubled over in pain, Covey

effect of not only weakening Hughes, but Covey also. When he saw Hughes bending over with pain, his courage quailed. He asked me if I meant to persist in my resistance. I told him I did, come what might; that he had used me like a brute for six months, and that I was determined to be used so no longer. With that, he strove to drag me to a stick that was lying just out of the stable door. He meant to knock me down. But just as he was leaning over to get the stick, I seized him with both hands by his collar, and brought him by a sudden snatch to the ground. By this time, Bill came. Covey called upon him for assistance. Bill wanted to know what he could do. Covey said, "Take hold of him, take hold of him!" Bill said his master hired him out to work, and not to help whip me; so he left Covey and myself to fight our own battle out. We

25 were at it for nearly two hours. Covey at length let me go, puffing and blowing at a great rate, saying that if I had not resisted, he would not have whipped me half so much. The truth was, that he had not whipped me at all. I considered him as getting entirely the worst end of the bargain; for he had drawn no blood from me, but I had from him. The whole six months afterwards, that I spent with Mr. Covey, he never laid the weight of his finger upon me in anger. He would occasionally say, he didn't want to get hold of me again. "No," thought I, "you need not; for you will come off worse than you did before."

26   This battle with Mr. Covey was the turning point in my career as a slave. It rekindled the few expiring embers of freedom, and revived within me a sense of my own manhood. It recalled the departed self-confidence, and inspired me again with a determination to be free. The gratification afforded by the triumph was a full compensation for whatever

lost some of his nerve. He asked me if I was going to keep fighting, and I said that I was. I told him he had used me like an animal for six months, and that I wouldn't allow it any longer. He tried to drag me to a stick that was lying outside the stable door. He wanted to knock me down. As he was leaning over to pick up the stick, I grabbed him by the collar with both hands and threw him onto the ground. Then Bill showed up, and Covey called for Bill to help him. Bill asked what he should do, and Covey said, "Hold him! Hold him!" Bill said that he had been hired to work, not to help whip me, and he left Covey and me to fight it out.

25   We kept at it for almost two hours. Covey finally let me go, huffing and puffing and saying that if I hadn't fought back, he would not have whipped me so hard. The truth was that he had not whipped me at all. He definitely got the bad end of the deal. He was bloody, and I was not. In the remaining six months that I served Covey, he never once laid a hand on me in anger. Once in a while he would say he didn't want to whip me again. "No," I thought," "you better not, or you will come out worse than you did before."

26   This fight with Mr. Covey was the turning point in my life as a slave. It relit the dying sparks of freedom within me and gave me a renewed sense of my own manhood. It brought back my confidence and made me once again determined to be free. The feeling of satisfaction I had was worth whatever I might pay, even death. Only he who has won a similar fight

else might follow, even death itself. He only can understand the deep satisfaction which I experienced, who has himself repelled by force the bloody arm of slavery. I felt as I never felt before. It was a glorious resurrection, from the tomb of slavery, to the heaven of freedom. My long-crushed spirit rose, cowardice departed, bold defiance took its place; and I now resolved that, however long I might remain slave in form, the day had passed forever when I could be a slave in fact. I did not hesitate to let it be known of me, that the white man who expected to succeed in whipping, must also succeed in killing me.

27   From this time I was never again what might be called fairly whipped, though I remained a slave four years afterwards. I had several fights, but was never whipped.

can understand the satisfaction I felt. I had risen from the death of slavery to the heaven of freedom. My broken and crushed spirit rose, and I would never be a coward again. I would always defy injustice. I promised myself that never again would I be a slave, despite my condition. I let everyone know that any white man who wanted to whip me must kill me first.

27   From that time on I was never again whipped, though I was a slave for four more years. I was in several fights, but I was never again whipped.

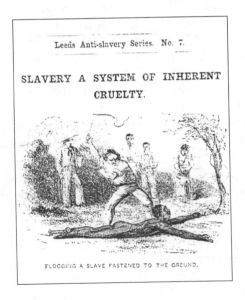

Leeds Anti-slavery Series. No. 7.

SLAVERY A SYSTEM OF INHERENT CRUELTY.

FLOGGING A SLAVE FASTENED TO THE GROUND.

The Gettysburg Address

Abraham Lincoln

1   *F*our score and seven years ago our fathers brought forth on this continent, a new nation, conceived in Liberty, and dedicated to the proposition that all men are created equal.

2   Now we are engaged in a great civil war, testing whether that nation, or any nation so conceived and so dedicated, can long endure. We are met on a great battlefield of that war. We have come to dedicate a portion of that field, as a final resting place for those who here gave their lives that this nation might live. It is altogether fitting and proper that we should do this.

3   But, in a larger sense, we can not dedicate—we can not consecrate—we can not hallow—this ground. The brave men, living and dead, who struggled here, have consecrated it, far above our poor power to add or detract.

The Gettysburg Address

Abraham Lincoln

Lincoln gave this address at the dedication of the battlefield at Gettysburg, Pennsylvania, on November 19, 1863. He used this speech to renew support for the war, which many thought was lasting far too long, and at too great a price.

1   Eighty-seven years ago our ancestors created a new nation on this continent. It was founded in liberty and dedicated to one ideal above all else—all men are created equal.

2   We are now in the middle of an enormous civil war. This war will decide whether our nation, or any nation based on and committed to this ideal, can survive. We are meeting on an important battlefield of that war. We have come to dedicate a part of the field as a final resting place for those who died so that the nation might live. It is the right thing to do.

3   But in a bigger way we cannot dedicate, honor, or make this ground holy. The brave men, living and dead, who fought here have made the ground holy far beyond our poor ability to do anything.

4   The world will little note, nor long remember what we say here, but it can never forget what they did here. It is for us the living, rather, to be dedicated here to the unfinished work which they who fought here have thus far so nobly advanced. It is rather for us to be here dedicated to the great task remaining before us—that from these honored dead we take increased devotion to that cause for which they gave the last full measure of devotion—that we here highly resolve that these dead shall not have died in vain—that this nation, under God, shall have a new birth of freedom—and that government of the people, by the people, for the people, shall not perish from the earth.

4   The world will soon forget what we say here today. It will, however, never forget what these men did. Thus, it is our duty to continue the work that those who fought here began. We must pledge ourselves to the great task that remains before us. From these honored dead we must gain a renewed sense of loyalty to the cause for which they gave their lives. These men must not have died in vain. This nation, under God, must have a new birth of freedom. The people's government—a government created by, controlled by, and devoted to its people—must not disappear from the earth.

Farewell to the Army

Robert E. Lee

1   *A*fter four years of arduous service, marked by
    unsurpassed courage and fortitude, the Army
    of Northern Virginia has been compelled to
yield to overwhelming numbers and resources. I need

2   not tell the survivors of so many hard-fought battles,
    who have remained steadfast to the last, that I con-
    sented to this result from no distrust of them; but

3   feeling that valor and devotion could accomplish
    nothing that would compensate for the loss that
    would have attended the continuation of the contest,

Farewell to the Army

Robert E. Lee

1   The Army of Northern Virginia has been forced
to surrender to a much larger and better-
equipped army. This surrender comes after
four years of dedicated service, marked by great
courage and persistence.

2   I want you, the brave survivors of so many difficult battles, who have stayed loyal to the end, to
know that I have not surrendered because I lack confidence in you.

3   Your bravery and loyalty would accomplish nothing worth the loss of life that would occur if we
continued this war. I do not want to sacrifice the lives

I determined to avoid the useless sacrifice of those whose past services have endeared them to their countrymen.

4   By the terms of the agreement, officers and men can return to their homes and remain there until exchanged. You will take with you the satisfaction that proceeds from the consciousness of duty faithfully performed; and I earnestly pray that a merciful God will extend to you His blessing and protection.

5   With an increasing admiration of your constancy and devotion to your country, and a grateful remembrance of your kind and generous consideration of myself, I bid you an affectionate farewell.

of those men who have served so well and are most precious to our country.

4   According to the agreement, officers and soldiers can return home and remain until exchanged. Take with you the satisfaction of knowing you have done your best. I pray that God in his mercy will bless and protect you.

5   I have come to admire your loyalty and devotion to your country. I am grateful for the many kindnesses you have shown me. With the greatest affection, I bid you farewell.

MAX LUCADO

EL ESPEJO DE DIOS

UNA PARÁBOLA ACTUAL

Reflejar el corazón
del Padre

MAX LUCADO

EL ESPEJO DE DIOS

UNA PARÁBOLA ACTUAL

CASA CREACIÓN
A STRANG COMPANY

*Reflejar el corazón
del Padre*

EL ESPEJO DE DIOS por Max Lucado
Publicado por Casa Creación
Una compañía de Strang Communications
600 Rinehart Road
Lake Mary, Florida 32746
www.casacreacion.com

A menos que se indique lo contrario, todos los textos bíblicos han sido tomados de la versión Reina-Valera, de la Santa Biblia, revisión 1960. Usado con permiso. Algunos textos bíblicos han sido tomados de la Santa Biblia, Nueva Versión Internacional (NVI), © 1999 por la Sociedad Bíblica Internacional. Usado con permiso.

Información del CD: *El espejo de Dios* es narrado por Danilo Montero. Producido por Casa Creación. Copyright © 2006 por Casa Creación. Todos los derechos reservados. La reproducción sin autorización es una violación a las leyes establecidas. "Tu misericordia", letra de Jacobo Ramos y cantada por Danilo Montero. Copyright © and ℗ 2005 Sigueme Internacional, Inc. Todos los derechos reservados.

Este libro fue publicado originalmente en los E.U.A. por Integrity Publishers, Inc.,
Brentwood, Tennessee, E.U.A.
bajo el título: *God's Mirror*
Copyright © 2005 by Max Lucado
Todos los derechos reservados
Traducido y usado con el permiso de Integrity Publishers, Inc.

Traducido por Belmonte Traductores
Diseño interior y portada por DeAnna Pierce, Mark Mickel/Brand Navigation, LLC.
Fotografía de portada por Getty Images and Veer

Library of Congress Control Number: 2006924640
ISBN: 1-59185-931-X

Impreso en China
06 07 08 09 10 — 9 8 7 6 5 4 3 2 1

PRIMERA PARTE

REFLEJAR SU CORAZÓN

"*¿Así que le gustan los*

ESCRITORES JUDÍOS?"

1

REFLEJAR SU CORAZÓN

"¿Así que le gustan los 'escritores judíos'?"

El hombre que planteaba la pregunta estaba sentado en el asiento de pasillo del avión. Yo estaba sentado próximo a la ventanilla, lo cual significaba que podía ver la pista de aterrizaje. Los mecánicos estaban reparando una abolladura causada por un pájaro en el ala. Mientras ellos trabajaban, yo leía. Mientras yo leía mi Biblia, el rabino me interrumpió.

"¿Así que le gustan los 'escritores judíos'?"

El brillo en sus ojos revelaba su placer en la pregunta. Su barba melenuda, que le llegaba al pecho, no podía esconder su sonrisa. De hecho, lo había notado antes en la zona de espera. Las borlas del faldón de su camisa y su sombrero sujeto al cabello me habían conducido a encasillarlo como el tipo de persona piadosa y silenciosa.

Piadosa. Sí. ¿Pero silenciosa? Le encantaba hablar. Le encantaba hablar de la Torá. Me esperaba una lección.

ESCONDIDOS *en las* CEREMONIAS
y las LEYES *de* MOISÉS *hay*
CUADROS *de* DIOS.

"Escondidos en las ceremonias y las leyes de Moisés," explicaba él, "hay cuadros de Dios." "¿Quién podría leer acerca de los siervos que redimen a sus parientes y no pensar en Dios redimiéndonos a nosotros? ¿Y quién podría leer el tercer mandamiento sin recordar vivir para la gloria de Dios?"

Hice una señal de pausa, abrí el libro de Éxodo y leí el tercer mandamiento:

"No TOMARÁS *el* NOMBRE *de*
JEHOVÁ *tu* DIOS *en* VANO . . . "

ÉXODO 20:7

Mi perplejidad fue suficiente para pedir una explicación.

"No piense en el lenguaje; piense en el estilo de vida", dijo él. "El mandamiento nos llama a elevar el nombre o reputación de Dios hasta el más alto lugar. Existimos para dar honor a su nombre. ¿Puedo poner un ejemplo?"

En aquel momento, el ala dañada quedó arreglada (la del avión; no puedo hablar por la del pájaro). Y a medida que íbamos ganando altitud, lo mismo hacía el rabino.

EXISTIMOS *para* DAR HONOR

a SU NOMBRE.

Yo tomaba notas, y él procedió a crear una historia acerca de un rascacielos de Manhattan. Todo el mundo en el edificio trabaja para el Director General, que tiene su oficina en el piso más alto. La mayoría de ellos nunca le ha visto, pero ha visto a su hija. Ella trabaja en el edificio para su papá. Y explota su posición familiar para beneficio propio.

Una mañana, ella se acerca a Bert, el guarda de seguridad. "Tengo hambre, Bert. Baja y cómprame un panecillo."

La demanda pone a Bert en un dilema. Él está de servicio, y dejar su puesto pone en riesgo al edificio. Pero la hija de su jefe insiste. "Vamos, ahora; apresúrate."

¿Qué opciones tiene él? A la vez que se aleja no dice nada, pero piensa algo parecido a:

SI *la* HIJA *es* TAN MANDONA,

¿QUÉ *se puede esperar de* SU PADRE?

Ella sólo acaba de empezar. Aún masticando su pastel, se topa con una secretaria cargada de papeles. "¿Dónde vas con todos esos papeles?"

"A prepararlos para la reunión de esta tarde."

"Olvida la reunión. Ven a mi oficina y limpia la alfombra."

"Pero me dijeron..."

"Y yo te digo otra cosa", interrumpió ella.

La mujer no tiene elección. Después de todo, le está hablando la hija del jefe. Lo cual hace que la secretaria se cuestione la sabiduría del jefe.

Y así sigue la hija. Haciendo demandas. Mandando. Interrumpiendo horarios. Nunca invocando el nombre de su papá. Nunca influyendo sus comentarios con: "Mi papá dijo...".

No tiene necesidad de hacerlo.

¿No es ella la hija del jefe? ¿No habla la hija por el padre? Y Bert, entonces, abandona su puesto. Una asistente no termina su tarea. Y más de un empleado se cuestiona la sabiduría del hombre que está en el piso de arriba.

¿Realmente sabe él lo que hace?, se preguntan ellos.

El rabino se detuvo en este punto. Ambos sentimos que el avión se inclinaba hacia delante. El tiempo que le quedaba era poco, pero el punto estaba claro. La muchacha deshonró el nombre de su padre no con un lenguaje vulgar, sino con una forma de vida insensible.

SI ESTO SIGUE ASÍ, *todo el* EDIFICIO

estará CRITICANDO

al DIRECTOR GENERAL.

Pero mi compañero de viaje no había terminado, y propuso: "¿Pero y si la hija actuase de manera diferente?", y entonces procedió a cambiar la historia.

En lugar de demandar a Bert que le trajera un panecillo, es ella quien le trae uno a Bert. "Esta mañana pensé en ti", le explica ella. "Llegas muy temprano; ¿tienes tiempo para comer?" Y le entrega el regalo.

De camino al ascensor se topa con una mujer que lleva los brazos llenos de documentos. "Vaya, lo siento, ¿puedo ayudarla?", se ofrece la hija. La asistente sonríe, y las dos cargan el montón por el pasillo.

Y así, la hija capta la atención de la gente. Ella pregunta por sus familias y se ofrece para llevarles café. Los trabajadores nuevos son bienvenidos, y los que trabajan duro son aplaudidos. Ella, a través de la amabilidad y la preocupación, eleva el nivel de felicidad de la empresa entera.

Ella hace esto aun sin mencionar el nombre de su papá. Nunca declara: "Mi papá dice...". No tiene necesidad de hacerlo. ¿No es ella su hija? ¿No habla en su nombre? ¿No refleja el corazón de él?

Cuando ella habla, ellos suponen que habla por
él. Y debido a que piensan bien de ella, piensan
bien de su padre.

Ellos no le han visto.

Ellos no le han conocido.

Pero conocen a su hija y, por tanto, conocen su
corazón.

ELLOS NO LE *han visto.*
ELLOS NO LE *han* CONOCIDO.
PERO *conocen a* SU HIJA *y,*
POR TANTO, *conocen* SU CORAZÓN.

Para entonces el vuelo estaba llegando a su fin, y también lo estaba mi lección de hebreo. Gracias al rabino, el tercer mandamiento cobró un nuevo significado. Pablo, otro rabino, habría apreciado ese punto. Él escribió:

"SOMOS EMBAJADORES *en nombre de* CRISTO, COMO SI DIOS ROGASE *por* MEDIO DE NOSOTROS ..." 2 CORINTIOS 5:20

EL EMBAJADOR *tiene una*

META SINGULAR:

REPRESENTAR *a su* REY.

Él anuncia la agenda del rey, protege la reputación del rey y presenta la voluntad del rey. El embajador eleva el nombre del rey.

Mi oración es que nosotros hagamos lo mismo. Que Dios nos rescate del pensamiento centrado en nosotros mismos. Que no tengamos una meta mayor que la de ver que alguien tenga un mejor concepto de nuestro Padre, nuestro Rey.

"¿Sabe usted cómo termina la historia?", preguntó el rabino a la vez que deteníamos a un taxi. Según parecía, tenía un buen final.

"No, no lo sé. ¿Cómo?"

"La hija se sube al ascensor y va hasta el piso más alto para ver a su papá. Cuando llega, él la está esperando en la puerta. Él está al tanto de sus buenas obras y ha visto sus actos de bondad. La gente tiene un mejor concepto de él debido a ella; y él lo sabe. A medida que ella se aproxima, él la saluda con seis palabras."

El rabino hizo una pausa y sonrió.

"¿Cuáles son?", insistí, sin esperar nunca escuchar a un judío ortodoxo citar a Jesús.

"Bien hecho, buen siervo y fiel."

QUE *el* CORAZÓN DEL PADRE

SE REFLEJE *así en usted para que*

ESCUCHE *lo* MISMO.

"Bien hecho, buen siervo *y* fiel."

Mateo 25:23 (NVI)

REFLEJAR
SU GLORIA

Ésta PODRÍA *ser* SU ÚNICA

POSIBILIDAD *de* ESCAPE.

G. R. Tweed miró a través de las aguas del Pacífico al barco estadounidense que se divisaba en el horizonte. Quitándose el sudor de jungla de sus ojos, el joven oficial de marina tragó saliva y tomó su decisión. Aquella podría ser su única posibilidad de escape.

Tweed había estado escondido en Guam durante casi tres años. Cuando los japoneses ocuparon la isla en el año 1941, él se sumergió en la espesa maleza tropical. La supervivencia no había sido fácil, pero él prefería el pantano en lugar de un campo de prisioneros de guerra.

La tarde del 10 de julio de 1944, él divisó la embarcación amistosa. Se apresuró a subir una colina y se situó en lo alto del precipicio. Metiendo la mano en su mochila, sacó un pequeño espejo. A las 6:20 de la tarde comenzó a enviar señales. Sujetando el extremo del espejo con sus dedos, lo inclinó hacia delante y hacia atrás, haciendo rebotar los rayos del sol en dirección al barco. Tres destellos cortos. Tres largos. De nuevo tres cortos. Punto-punto-punto. Raya-raya-raya. Punto-punto-punto. SOS.

Tres DESTELLOS CORTOS.

Tres LARGOS. *Tres* CORTOS

DE NUEVO. SOS

La señal captó la mirada de un marinero a bordo del USS *McCall*. Un grupo de rescate subió a bordo de una lancha a motor, y llegó sigilosamente a la ensenada, fuera de la zona de tiro. Tweed fue rescatado.

Él se alegró de tener ese espejo, se alegró de saber cómo usarlo, y se alegró de que el espejo cooperase. Supongamos que no lo hubiera hecho (prepárese para una idea disparatada). Supongamos que el espejo se hubiera resistido, imponiendo sus propios planes. En lugar de reflejar un mensaje del sol, supongamos que hubiera optado por enviar el suyo propio.

SUPONGAMOS *que el* ESPEJO

se hubiera RESISTIDO,

imponiendo SUS PROPIOS PLANES.

Después de todo, tres años de aislamiento habría dejado a cualquiera muriéndose por recibir atención. En lugar de enviar un SOS, el espejo podría haber enviado un MAM: "Mírame a mí".

¿Un espejo egoísta?

La única idea más disparatada aún sería la de un espejo inseguro. *¿Y si lo echo todo a perder? ¿Y si envío una raya cuando se supone que debo enviar un punto? Además, ¿has visto las manchas de mi superficie?* La desconfianza en sí mismo podría paralizar a un espejo.

LA DESCONFIANZA EN SÍ MISMO

podría PARALIZAR *a un* ESPEJO.

Y lo mismo podría hacer la autocompasión. *Haber estado metido en esa mochila, arrastrado por la jungla, ¿y ahora, de repente, se espera que me enfrente al brillante sol y realice un servicio crucial? De ninguna manera. Mejor me quedo en la mochila. Que de mí no salga ningún reflejo.*

Fue muy bueno que el espejo de Tweed no tuviera una mente propia.

¿Pero los espejos de Dios? Lamentablemente, la tenemos.

Nosotros somos sus espejos; herramientas de la

heliografía celestial. Reduzcamos a una sola frase la descripción de trabajo de los humanos, y será esta: Reflejar la gloria de Dios.

Como Pablo escribió:

"Así TODOS NOSOTROS, *que* CON EL ROSTRO DESCUBIERTO REFLEJAMOS COMO EN UN ESPEJO *la* GLORIA *del* SEÑOR, SOMOS TRANSFORMADOS *a su* SEMEJANZA CON MÁS Y MÁS GLORIA *por la acción del* SEÑOR, *que es el* ESPÍRITU."

2 CORINTIOS 3:18 (NVI)

Reflejar LA GLORIA DE DIOS.

Algún lector acaba de arquear una ceja. *Un momento*, está usted pensando, *yo ya he leído ese pasaje anteriormente, y más de una vez. Y ha sonado distinto*. Y puede que, efectivamente, así haya sido. Quizá es porque usted está acostumbrado a leerlo en una versión diferente. "Por tanto, nosotros todos, *mirando* a cara descubierta *como en un espejo* la gloria del Señor, somos transformados de gloria en gloria en la misma imagen, como por el Espíritu del Señor" (énfasis mío).

EL ESPEJO DE DIOS

Una traducción dice: "contemplando como en un espejo"; otra dice: "reflejamos como en un espejo". Una implica contemplación; la otra implica refracción. ¿Cuál de ellas es fiel y exacta?

En realidad, ambas lo son. El verbo *katoptrizo* puede traducirse de las dos maneras. Hay traductores en ambos bandos:

"*reflejando* como en un espejo" (RVR)

"*contemplando* como en un espejo" (LBLA)

"*mirando* ... como en un espejo" (RV–60)

"*reflejamos* como en un espejo" (NVI)

"somos como un espejo *que refleja la grandeza del Señor*" (DHH)

¿Pero cuál de los significados quería Pablo expresar? En el contexto del pasaje, Pablo comparaba la experiencia cristiana con la experiencia de Moisés en el monte Sinaí. Después de que el patriarca hubo *contemplado* la gloria de Dios, su rostro *reflejaba* la gloria de Dios. "Los hijos de Israel no pudieron fijar la vista en el rostro de Moisés a causa de la gloria de su rostro" (2 Corintios 3:7).

El rostro de Moisés era de un blanco tan deslumbrante que "los israelitas no podían mirar la cara de Moisés debido a la gloria que se reflejaba en su rostro" (2 Corintios 3:7 NVI).

Al contemplar a Dios, Moisés no pudo evitar sino reflejar a Dios. *El resplandor que él vio fue el resplandor en el cual se convirtió.* Contemplar conduce a convertirse, y convertirse conduce a reflejar. Quizá la respuesta a la pregunta sobre la traducción, por tanto, sea "sí".

¿Quiso Pablo decir "mirando como en un espejo"? Sí.

El RESPLANDOR QUE ÉL VIO
fue el RESPLANDOR EN EL
CUAL SE CONVIRTIÓ.

¿Quiso Pablo decir "reflejamos como en un espejo"? Sí.

¿Podría ser que el Espíritu Santo seleccionó intencionadamente un verbo que nos recordase que hiciésemos ambas cosas? ¿Que contemplemos a Dios tan fijamente que no podamos evitar sino reflejarlo?

¿Qué significa contemplar nuestro rostro en un espejo? ¿Una mirada rápida? ¿Un vistazo casual? No. Contemplar es mirar fijamente, observar, examinar. Contemplar la gloria de Dios, entonces, no es una mirada pasajera o un vistazo ocasional; contemplar es una meditación seria.

DESTELLOS *de la* GLORIA *de* DIOS...

¿No es eso lo que hemos hecho? Hemos acampado al pie del monte Sinaí y hemos contemplado la gloria de Dios. Sabiduría inescrutable. Pureza sin mancha. Años infinitos. Fuerza inmutable. Amor sin medida. Destellos de la gloria de Dios.

A medida que contemplamos su gloria, ¿nos atrevemos a orar para que nosotros, al igual que Moisés, la reflejemos? ¿Nos atrevemos a ser espejos en las manos de Dios, en el reflejo de la luz divina? Este es el llamado.

"*Hacedlo* TODO PARA *la* GLORIA *de* DIOS."

1 CORINTIOS 10:31

TODO. TODO.

QUE SU MENSAJE
REFLEJE LA GLORIA DE DIOS.

"*Hagan* BRILLAR SU LUZ *delante de*
TODOS,
para que ELLOS *puedan* VER LAS BUENAS
OBRAS DE USTEDES *y* ALABEN AL
PADRE *que está en* EL CIELO."

MATEO 5:16 (NVI)

QUE SU SALVACIÓN REFLEJE LA GLORIA DE DIOS.

"... *y* LO CREYERON, FUERON MARCADOS CON *el* SELLO *que es el* ESPÍRITU SANTO PROMETIDO. ÉSTE GARANTIZA *nuestra* HERENCIA HASTA QUE LLEGUE LA REDENCIÓN FINAL *del* PUEBLO ADQUIRIDO POR DIOS, *para* ALABANZA DE SU GLORIA".

EFESIOS 1:13–14 (NVI)

QUE SU CUERPO REFLEJE LA GLORIA DE DIOS.

"¿ . . . Y *que* NO *sois* VUESTROS? . . .

GLORIFICAD, *pues*, A DIOS

EN VUESTRO CUERPO . . . "

1 CORINTIOS 6:19–20

SUS LUCHAS DAN HONRA A DIOS.

"TODAS ESTAS COSAS PADECEMOS
POR AMOR A VOSOTROS, *para que*
ABUNDANDO LA GRACIA *por medio*
DE MUCHOS, *la* ACCIÓN DE GRACIAS
sobreabunde PARA GLORIA DE DIOS".

2 CORINTIOS 4:15 (RVR); VER TAMBIÉN JUAN 11:4

SU ÉXITO DA HONRA A DIOS.

"HONRA *al* SEÑOR *con tus* RIQUEZAS..."

PROVERBIOS 3:9 (NVI)

"LAS RIQUEZAS *y la* GLORIA PROCEDEN *de* TI."

1 CRÓNICAS 29:12

"DIOS... *te* DÉ EL PODER PARA HACER

LAS RIQUEZAS..."

DEUTERONOMIO 8:18

El mensaje, la salvación, el cuerpo, las luchas, los éxitos suyos: todo ello proclama la gloria de Dios.

———

"Y TODO LO QUE HACÉIS, *sea de* PALABRA *o de* HECHO, HACEDLO TODO *en el* NOMBRE *del* SEÑOR JESÚS, DANDO GRACIAS *a* DIOS PADRE POR MEDIO DE ÉL".

COLOSENSES 3:17

Él es la fuente; nosotros somos el cristal. Él es la luz; nosotros somos los espejos. Él envía el mensaje; nosotros lo reflejamos. Descansamos dentro de su mochila, esperando su llamado. Y cuando estamos colocados en sus manos, hacemos su obra. No se trata de nosotros; todo se trata de Él.

El uso que el Sr. Tweed le dio al espejo condujo a un rescate.

Que el uso que Dios haga de nosotros conduzca a millones de rescates más.